FINANCING HIGHER EDUCATION

FINANCING HIGHER EDUCATION

The Public Investment

Edited by

JOHN C. HOY
MELVIN H. BERNSTEIN

New England Board of
Higher Education

 Auburn House Publishing Company
Boston, Massachusetts

Library of Congress Cataloging in Publication Data
Main entry under title:
Financing higher education.

   Includes index.
   1. Universities and colleges—New England—Finance—
Addresses, essays, lectures. I. Hoy, John C. II. Bern-
stein, Melvin H., 1934-   .
LB2342.F525 1982   379.1'224'0974   82–13733
ISBN 0-86569-114-2

Printed in the United States of America

FOREWORD

by Senator Robert J. McKenna

Public funding of higher education is an extremely important issue to New England and the nation which had not been adequately addressed in this region until the New England Board of Higher Education held its conference on tax policy in Boston early in 1982. The ideas presented at that gathering of legislators, businessmen, educators and journalists led to this collection of chapters on the issue of public investment in higher education. I believe that as a result of that conference, and of the public discussion and further research that it encouraged, we will gain a more sophisticated view of the future of higher education in New England and of the economy of the region.

In December of 1977, when John C. Hoy was being interviewed for the position of president of the New England Board, one of the questions I asked was, "Do you see any connection between higher education and the future development of the New England economy?" We knew of his energetic efforts in California on behalf of the relationship between higher education and economic development. Fortunately for the Board, and far more importantly for all of us in New England, he did see this connection for this six-state region and was committed to realizing its potential. Based on his bringing to fruition the Commission on Higher Education and the Economy of New England, which has so advanced our understanding of this connection in this region, our decision to offer him the presidency of the Board has been fully rewarded.

As Patricia F. Pannell observes in this volume, "Whatever weaknesses there may be in the region's economic base, a shortage of revenue per se does not appear to explain the low level of public resources available to higher education." Because of my activities as a state senator, I have learned the very important truth that, to a high degree, public policy makers, especially those on finance and appropriation committees, see higher education, particularly public higher education, as a very expensive item in state budgets.

When you are trying to save state funds, there is also a tendency to cut back or at least hold down the rate of increase in public support of public higher education, specifically, and in support of all higher education in general.

In my view, this does not produce a particularly desirable policy outcome, because when you cut back on higher education resources you also cut back on the possibilities for current and future economic development. Michael S. McPherson notes in his chapter, "The notion that education has the requisite characteristics of durability and productive value to define it as an investment has been around at least since Adam Smith, who cited 'the skill, dexterity, and judgment' of the labor force as one of the two great determinants of the 'wealth of nations.'"

It is important that we develop an adequate data base and a sound series of policy considerations which will be a guide to the policy-makers of New England. This group obviously includes governors and legislators. However, I believe college presidents and trustees, the business community, and the media must be partners to these deliberations. It is very important that we all have an understanding, hopefully a mutually agreed upon understanding, of the interconnection between higher education and the economy.

It was out of this concern that the New England Board of Higher Education created the Commission on Higher Education and the Economy of New England, chaired by James M. Howell, Senior Vice President and Chief Economist of the First National Bank of Boston. The Commission is composed of thirty-one distinguished New England representatives of business, government, academia, and labor and has been concerned with comprehensively examining the special role of colleges and universities in fostering the long-term prosperity of the New England economy. In its proceedings, the Commission has focused on two central issues. First, why should institutions of higher education want to help the economy of the region? Second, what can these institutions do to assist the economy of the region?

In addition, the Commission is concerned with the interface between academia and both private industry and government. We realize that this relationship involves perceptions and attitudes of each sector which can from time to time vitiate the effectiveness of the cooperative process. Thus a full understanding of the positive and negative aspects of current, established relationships is important. In March 1982 the Commission issued its report and recommendations, which are included as an appendix to this volume.

The conference on tax policy advanced the Commission's ultimate goal of determining the direct effect of government investment and distribution of tax revenues on the higher education sector and the indirect benefit such investment contributes to the economic vitality of the region. To satisfy this goal, the Commission is committed to the following objectives:

1. Developing an understanding of the state and local tax burden on present and future development of higher education, the chief resource of our knowledge-intensive regional economy.
2. Determining and revealing how higher education carries its fair share of economic responsibility under the present tax structure of the region.
3. Assessing the distribution of tax revenues in support of academic instruction, research and development, and public service.
4. Assessing the levels of tuition in contrast to general tax revenues in the region for both undergraduate and graduate programs, and studying related matters affecting public support of expanded access to higher education.

The searching analyses and provocative presentations offered by the authors of this volume bring us much closer, I believe, to satisfying these objectives of the Commission. This book completes a three-part series developed by the New England Board of Higher Education to investigate the relationship between higher education and the economy of New England. The first volume, *Business and Academia: Partners in New England's Economic Renewal* (University Press of New England, 1981), takes a hard look at the connection between business and academia. It argues that colleges can no longer take a self-righteous, parochial approach to relations with business and industry, but rather must cooperate effectively if both sectors are to maximize their resources. The second, *New England's Vital Resource: The Labor Force* (American Council on Education, 1982), extends further the New England model for a knowledge-intensive national economy, discussing the qualities requisite in an appropriate labor force.

I believe it is essential to put the public investment issue in a general context. I think that most of us who are educators believe that education is good in itself. It is a desirable thing; it makes for a better life. It enables each of us not only to live well in a satisfactory economic situation, but in fact makes us better citizens and persons. For that reason alone, it should be supported and developed.

However, I think from the standpoint of many policy-makers that good has to be balanced against competing public interests, such as the environment, welfare, transportation, and other pressing needs. But one area that over the past decade has received an increasingly positive response from policy-makers at the state level is the need for state involvement in economic development. Additional funds often can be obtained from the legislatures on a governor's recommendation because development strategies are likely to generate additional economic capacity within the state.

What we must now do is emphasize that higher education is not only good in itself, but also that, either in the short run or, more importantly, in the long run, investment in higher education must result in substantial augmentation of the economic base of a particular state and of the New England region. My own impression is that the value of the investment in higher education has not been fully understood intellectually and certainly not in terms of the emotion-laden response of legislators and governors when the chips are down and they must cope with a shortfall in taxes or an excess in expenditures in the state budget. Higher education is not one of the prime areas which is seen as essential, and which therefore should not be touched.

In his chapter economist Anthony Carnevale points out that between 1948 and 1979 human capital improvements represented a larger share of national productivity growth than did machine capital. He affirms that "in simplest terms a human capital strategy means more and better education and training." As the authors of this volume and of the previous two volumes in the series point out, education should be an economic priority in our region, as a skilled labor force is our most important resource. I do not wish to go into detail here about Rhode Island policy, but balancing conflicting priorities certainly has been the hallmark of legislative trade-offs in recent years. Perhaps some of the ideas presented here will help tip the balance a little further in the direction of public support for higher education.

I think that there are two key factors to consider in reading this book. The first is fiscal impact. What happens when state and local government funds are appropriated? How are they distributed? These are essentially fiscal policies at the state level. They are evaluated in great detail in this book. The second factor is the question of tax policy per se. Which tax policies in fact have a differential impact on higher education, and on those industries that are closely associated with higher education? For example: What is the policy on tax exemption? Connecticut has a reimbursement for tax-exempt property to the cities and towns. I think this option has an important effect on the receptivity of particular communities to the existence of higher education institutions in their environs. Other states could well emulate the Connecticut pattern.

We also need to examine the implications of recent changes in federal tax laws regarding the treatment of private sector contributions to higher education. If it is less advantageous to give money to higher education because of the change in the tax laws, what impact will this policy have on both the public and independent sectors of higher education in New England?

The book gives a very broad view of the national context of funding and the allocation of fiscal resources to higher education in New England. It is very important that we understand the national context. Editor Melvin H. Bernstein argues that at both national and regional levels, "Few of government's services produce as high a rate of return to the economy and society, as well as to the individual, as does public investment in higher education." We have to understand that New England is different from the rest of the country, but the question is, how different? And should we, in fact, be different in the ways that we are? We have to realize that to a very large extent, each individual state has been operating almost in a vacuum. What we do in Rhode Island seems to have little or no connection with what is legislated in the other New England states.

The region should seek to develop increasingly unified strategies. I believe that it is essential that we develop a deeper regional perspective and deliberately seek regional cooperation in many areas of economic development. President Jean Mayer of Tufts University comments that ". . . there is a considerable waste . . . in resources in the public sector due to duplication in each state of what should be devised for the economy of New England."

In fact, the New England Board of Higher Education was created more than a quarter of a century ago on the assumption that the six states would benefit from regional problem-solving in higher education. I think that was a sound idea twenty-six years ago. It is at least as sound an idea now, and it will become imperative to pursue this concept in the 1980s.

What *Financing Higher Education: The Public Investment* aims at, fundamentally, is the provision of policy guidance for those who will have to make the final decisions: the elected officials, the people in the various state departments of education, the boards of governors of higher education, and those in the academic and business communities.

PREFACE

In its report, *A Threat to Excellence*, the New England Board's Commission on Higher Education and the Economy of New England identified three regional imperatives: strengthening of secondary education in the region, enhancement of New England's image as an area of opportunity, and improvement of our regional capacity to finance higher education. The third point is of most direct concern to academics; it is also the most easily addressed by broad public policy decisions. Nevertheless, despite New England's historic commitment to higher education and its present dependence on training and research as a vital component of its economy, the six states have only just begun to respond to the challenges posed by economic dislocation, vigorous competition from other regions, and the withdrawal of federal leadership.

New England's public financial investment in higher education in recent years has been unimpressive. In part this reflects a heavy dependence on private institutions, but even our direct public spending on private higher education has been relatively small. Public higher education across the region has been underfunded by any criterion, including expenditure per enrolled student. New England has become a relatively poor region, and its public financial capacity is stretched to the limit. Higher education, if it is to continue its role as a "lead sector" in this regional economy, must not merely survive, not simply maintain its present strengths, but must increase its latitude for innovation. The various chapters in this book explore the dimensions of this challenge to public policy, identify the most critical problems, and sketch out approaches to their solution.

New England higher education has an unequalled tradition of quality, prestige, and stability. It has become an integral part of an economy that is a model for the knowledge-intensive twenty-first century world. Yet, its viability is threatened by irresolution and illogic in public policy—for which academic leaders must themselves shoulder much of the responsibility. In these respects, it differs only in degree from the American higher education system as a whole. Examination of New England's experience and prospects, then, brings into sharp relief problems and possibilities which may be blurred in a national perspective.

It is a basic assumption of this book that, for the foreseeable future, public policy initiatives in the field of higher education will emanate from the states and regions rather than from Washington. The authors have not, therefore, delved deeply into issues of federal tax policy and aid, except insofar as they place new demands upon other revenue sources or impinge upon state and local fiscal policy. Thus, for example, there is no discussion of Boston University President John Silber's Tuition Advance Fund proposal, a national plan relying on the Internal Revenue Service to collect student loan payments. Obviously, necessity being the mother of invention, we may expect to see other new approaches to financing higher education, many of them imaginative, some defying all categorization.

An example of such initiatives is the recent, well-publicized, and markedly successful bond issue by Dartmouth College, intended to fund both capital improvements and student aid. In this case, the bonds are backed by Dartmouth's strong credit rating but are issued through a state agency, the New Hampshire Higher Educational and Health Facilities Authority, so as to be exempt from federal income taxes. There is no commitment of state funds involved; New Hampshire has merely extended to Dartmouth the umbrella of its tax-exempt borrowing power, allowing the college to garner an indirect federal subsidy. Although the federal government had already begun efforts to restrict issuance of such bonds, many institutions of higher learning in other New England states and elsewhere are currently planning similar issues. Clearly, whatever the future of this particular ploy, such creative cooperation between state government and academia is essential to the survival of excellence in higher education.

We recognize that there cannot be a single New England policy toward public investment in higher education. Each of the six states must pursue its own policy. New England is nonetheless a real region, and New England higher education must, as other regional segments should also, identify common challenges and shape consistent policies to confront them.

JOHN C. HOY
MELVIN H. BERNSTEIN

ACKNOWLEDGMENTS

We are grateful to the distinguished foundations that have supported the final phase of the planning stage of the work of the Commission on Higher Education and the Economy of New England. The W. K. Kellogg Foundation through Arlon E. Elser, Program Director, and the Andrew Mellon Foundation through Claire List, Program Director, provided grants to support the studies, writing, conferences, and final report that define the issues and make recommendations for change in higher education so that it can contribute more effectively to the New England economy. The Calvin K. Kazanjian Economics Foundation through John C. Schramm, Managing Director, gave a gift to further the analysis of New England's economic needs and to disseminate the findings to business, government, and institutions of higher learning.

We are also indebted to the members of the Corporate Council who have supported the Commission's program. The leadership demonstrated by these corporations has given the Commission latitude in shaping its investigations to consider timely economic issues confronting New England. The members of the Corporate Council include: The Barnes Group, Inc.; The Continental Group, Inc.; The Digital Equipment Corporation; The First National Bank of Boston; General Electric Foundation; Germanium Power Devices Corporation; The Hartford Insurance Group; The Raytheon Company; The Rogers Corporation; Sanders Associates, Inc.; and Wheelabrator Frye, Inc.

Senator Robert J. McKenna of the Rhode Island Legislature, as Chairman of the Tax Policy Task Force of the Commission, has strongly supported the development of new ideas and data which clarify the financial condition of higher education in New England. We further wish to acknowledge our gratitude to James M. Howell of the First National Bank of Boston and Chairman of the Commission for his vigorous leadership, counsel, and insights. Robert W. Eisenmenger of the Federal Reserve Bank of Boston wisely recommended Dr. Howell for the Commission Chairmanship and has in turn been a steady source of guidance and support in our efforts. Francis Keppel and Sidney P. Marland, Jr., both former United States Commissioners of Education, have given us the benefits of their perspective and wide-ranging knowledge in our discussions. Robert E. Miller, Chairman of the New England Board of Higher Education, has been a staunch supporter throughout in presenting the ideas of this book in published form.

D. Kent Halstead of the National Institute of Education and Marilyn McCoy, formerly of the National Center for Higher Education Management Systems, graciously provided advance copies of valuable comparative national data that put New England's financial support of higher education into clearer perspective.

Finally, the editors wish to express their appreciation to Terry Hill for her skillful production editing, to Anne Marie Delaney for valuable research support, and to Nancy Balf for her efficient administrative assistance.

JOHN C. HOY
MELVIN H. BERNSTEIN

ABOUT THE AUTHORS

MELVIN H. BERNSTEIN is Vice President for Research and Development for the New England Board of Higher Education. He is editor and co-author of the three-part series of which this is the third volume. The other two books are *Business and Academia* and *New England's Vital Resource: The Labor Force*.

ANTHONY P. CARNEVALE is Consulting Economist to the American Society for Training and Development. Based in Washington, he has acted as policy analyst for federal agencies, congressional committees, and labor organizations.

WARD S. CURRAN is Professor of Economics and George M. Ferris Lecturer in Corporation Finance at Trinity College. He is the author of *Principles of Financial Management*.

ROBERT W. EISENMENGER is Senior Vice President and Director of Research at the Federal Reserve Bank of Boston. He is the author of *The Dynamics of Growth in New England's Economy, 1870–1964*.

JOHN C. HOY is President of the New England Board of Higher Education. He is editor and co-author (with Melvin Bernstein) of the three-part series of which this is the third volume.

JEAN MAYER is President of Tufts University. He is a world-renowned nutritionist and served as chairman of the White House Conference on Food, Nutrition and Health.

ROBERT J. MCKENNA is a state senator of Rhode Island and Professor of History and Politics at Salve Regina: The Newport College. He is chairman of the Finance Committee of the Rhode Island Senate.

MICHAEL S. MCPHERSON is Associate Professor of Economics at Williams College. His contribution to this volume was written during a year spent at the Institute for Advanced Study of Princeton University.

JOANN MOODY is Director of Intergovernmental Relations for the New England Board of Higher Education. She is a member of the Massachusetts Bar and a former associate professor of English and American studies at Lynchburg College.

PATRICIA F. PANNELL is Assistant Professor of Economics at Bentley College and Research Associate of the Institute for Employment Policy of Boston University. She has contributed to each of the three volumes in this series.

CONTENTS

FINANCING HIGHER EDUCATION

Chapter 1

UNDERFUNDING AND OVERTAXING IN NEW ENGLAND

by Melvin H. Bernstein

New England is shortchanging its system of higher education. Dependent for so long on the earliest and most developed concentration of private colleges and universities in the nation, the region now finds that it cannot maintain its preeminent position without committing more public resources to higher education. Enough facts and indicators have become available for the first time to get a reasonably clear financial picture of the condition of higher education in New England and each of its six states when compared with the rest of the United States. The picture suggests government in the region must reassess its funding priorities if it wishes to advance the cause of economic progress and productivity in a knowledge-intensive economy heavily reliant on the manpower and technology transfer produced by higher education.

Overall, I find no comprehensive reasonably current studies of taxes and tax policy for New England. Much of the tax information is found in chapters of older books on the regional economy, in more recent national studies, in official reports of the six state governments, and in articles written for periodicals such as the *Chronicle of Higher Education* and the *New England Economic Review* of the Federal Reserve Bank of Boston. Still less literature exists on financial support of state government for higher education in the region. Only recently has the work of D. Kent Halstead at the National Institute of Education made possible the extraction

1

of data required for analysis of each of the New England states, the region, and the nation.[1] Professor Ward Curran's innovative research presented in Chapter 5 contributes greatly to measuring the higher education factor in regional and national gross domestic products.

For too long government has regarded funding of higher education as an expense. That view is changing as more and more government decision-makers realize that it is an investment which contributes directly and indirectly to the health and competitiveness of the economy. Government officials are not the only ones who have been slow in coming around to this realization. Higher education, with few exceptions, has not made a cogent case to persuade the public and its elected representatives that investment in higher education produces concrete results for the economy. Few of government's services produce as high a rate of return to the economy and society, as well as to the individual, as does public investment in higher education. More will be said about the rate of return at the end of the chapter, but first let us consider a few financial facts showing why higher education is big business in New England:

- New England's gross regional product is 5.2 percent of gross national product, but New England's higher education financial share of national higher education is 7.2 percent (nearly 40 percent higher).[2]
- Higher education will have direct expenditures of $5 billion for fiscal year 1982.[3]
- Physical plant assets of higher education amount to $5.3 billion at book value.
- Endowment assets of higher education total $3.7 billion at market value.
- Federal contract and grant money for research brought into the region by higher education totals $560 million.[4]

Considering that New England is a region impoverished by lack of natural resources, with the exception of brain power, higher education is a major economic resource whose full potential is yet to be realized. Continuing the underfunded condition of public higher education in the region will make it difficult to achieve that potential.

Government's Track Record in Funding Higher Education

That New England has underfunded public higher education is demonstrated in Table 1–1, which shows the five-year trend for state and local tax appropriations. The percentages for the six states compared with the national averages indicate the relatively low importance assigned to financing public higher education in the government budgets. All New England states rank in the bottom fifth of the 50 states of the Union and the District of Columbia. There has been little change over the five-year period. Massachusetts, the lowest-ranked state in 1982, stood last in 1978 also. Rhode Island, highest ranking of all New England states, finishes 40th for 1982, as it did in 1978.

In looking at funding of public higher education in relation to dollars spent per capita or per student, we also see little change. New England's support still falls much below national norms:

Appropriations per capita	*1981–1982*
United States	$101.21
New England	$ 67.61

According to the per capita measure, all New England states appropriate substantially less money to higher education than the national average. Only Rhode Island and Connecticut come reasonably close at $90.03 and $83.65, respectively. New Hampshire finishes last in the region and last in the nation at $42.70.

Finally, should there be any doubt, the dollars-spent-per-student indicator shows clearly New England's pattern of underfunding public higher education:

Appropriations per student	*1980–1981*
United States	$3,498
New England	$2,746

The New England states spend *$752 less per student* for public higher education than the national average. All New England states except Connecticut rank below the national average for

Table 1–1 **Allocation of State and Local Tax Revenues to Public Higher Education**

State	FY 78		FY 79		FY 80		FY 81		FY 82	
	Percent	*Rank*	*Percent*	*Rank*	*Percent*	*Rank*	*Percent*	*Rank*	*Percent*	*Rank*
Conn.	6.6	45	8	43	7.2	43	8.4	42	7.9	44
Maine	6.3	48	7	47	6.9	46	7.5	45	7.6	47
Mass.	4.8	51	6	50	5.1	51	4.9	51	5.0	51
N.H.	5.9	50	8	44	5.1	50	5.6	50	6.2	49
R.I.	9.1	40	9	40	9.0	39	9.3	39	9.2	40
Vt.	6.6	46	8	46	6.6	47	7.5	44	8.0	43
U.S.	10.6		11		10.4		11.3		10.8	

SOURCE: Compiled from published and unpublished data of the National Institute of Education and the National Center for Higher Education Management Systems.

dollars spent per student. Connecticut appropriates $3,894 per student, advancing to a national ranking of 12th under this measure. This is accounted for in part by the fact that, although Connecticut's allocation of tax revenue to higher education is one of the lowest in the country, its enrollments are low also, resulting in higher appropriations per student. Rhode Island is the only other state in the region moving up—from the bottom fifth of all states to 32nd place at $3,297 per student. It, too, has lower enrollments per 1,000 population than the U.S. average, which helps to explain the improvement in ranking. New Hampshire again finishes last at $1,695.

Furthermore, New England as a whole ranks well below the national norm for state and local funding as a proportion of all revenue generated by public higher education. While the national average is 59 percent, New England states provide only 50 percent of the revenue received by its colleges and universities. Massachusetts at 70 percent and Connecticut at 64 percent exceed both regional and national averages for government appropriations to higher education institutions. In these two largest of the New England states, government appropriations make up more of the institutional revenues because there is less reliance on student tuition and on grants and contracts, which are below national averages. On the other hand, the three northern states and Rhode Island rely more heavily on tuition and on grants and contracts, which are above the national average.[5]

Vision is Needed

New England, along with the South and the West, is projected to gain jobs between now and 1985. That growth is expected largely from expansion of high technology industries and related sophisticated professional services. The top four states in the nation ranked by importance of high technology employment are all in New England: New Hampshire, Massachusetts, Vermont, and Connecticut, in that order.[6] Economic growth in these high technology states is tied to higher education productivity of manpower and research and development. Recognizing the opportunities for economic progress, the sunbelt states most competitive with New England in technology are pouring huge sums into public higher education. North Carolina, for example, with per capita personal income of only $7,852, ranks 41st nationally, but it ranks as high as 4th in allocating 17.5 percent of its state budget to public higher education. North Carolina ranks 16th in high technology employment and promises to move up rapidly.[7] Massachusetts, on the other hand, has a high per capita income of $9,992, ranking 13th nationally, but it allocates only 5 percent of its state budget to public higher education, ranking 51st—at the bottom of the heap.

Economic progress in the 1980s in large measure means technology growth, particularly in a knowledge-intensive economy such as New England. A major obstacle to realizing potential growth is the paucity of funding for public higher education in New England, which now accounts for over 50 percent of all college and university enrollments in the region.

Excessive Tax Burdens in New England

Though New England states compare poorly with national norms in funding of public higher education, it seems unrealistic to expect that taxes will be raised to remedy this limitation on a resource vital to the regional economy. The state and national movement which began in the late seventies to reduce taxes, or at least hold the line, has produced Proposition 13 in California, Proposition 2½ in Massachusetts, and historic federal tax cuts. The national mood remains opposed to increasing direct taxes and the very idea of raising taxes in an election year is anathema to politicians.

A brief review of the level of taxes in New England shows that taxes have been more burdensome in the region than for most other states. However, when considering the tax burden, the tax capacity of states as well as their tax efforts should be taken into account.

First, as to tax capacity, which involves the potential of government to raise revenue by applying national average tax rates to its tax base, the average for all American states is $986.50 per capita. Connecticut at $1,035.90, the wealthiest state in New England, is the only state in the region with a tax capacity above the national average. (See Table 1–2.)

Second, for tax effort—meaning revenue actually collected as a percentage of government capacity—all New England states but New Hampshire, at 72.7 percent, make an effort above the na-

Table 1–2 Tax Capacity and Tax Effort, New England and the United States, 1980

State	Tax Capacity ($ per capita)	Tax Effort (percent)
Conn.	$1,035.90	102.3%
Mass.	897.80	137.1
Maine	779.40	108.5
N.H.	947.10	72.7
R.I.	818.90	119.1
Vt.	828.80	101.1
U.S.	986.50	100.0

SOURCE: D. Kent Halstead, "How States Compare in Financial Support of Higher Education, 1981–1982" (Washington, D.C.: National Institute of Education, February 11, 1982).

tional norm of 100 percent. Massachusetts at 137.1 percent and Rhode Island at 119.1 percent substantially exceed the tax effort norm while Connecticut, the state with the largest tax capacity, barely makes an effort above the national average.

As shown in the following table, state and local governments in New England, led by Massachusetts, tax more heavily than the national norm.[8] The exceptions are Connecticut, which does not have an income tax, and New Hampshire, which has neither an income nor a sales tax.

Taxes Relative to Personal Income	
United States	100%
New England	109%
Connecticut	95%
Maine	107%
Massachusetts	123%
New Hampshire	83%
Rhode Island	108%
Vermont	117%

We have seen that New England as a region has a tax capacity lower than the national norm. However, although it is poorer than most regions, it makes a greater effort to tax than its potential indicates. In a region that already taxes high relative to its financial capacity it is fair to say that increases in support for higher education are unlikely to come from increased taxes for the immediate future.

Assessing the Business Climate in New England

The significance of the tax burden to the health of the economy is an issue that has confronted New England since World War II. Little had changed until the 1970s when high technology industries emerged as a major growth force in the region and then entered into fierce competition with companies in such states as California, Texas, North Carolina, Arizona, Colorado, and Florida. Then in 1980 in Massachusetts, the bellwether state of New England, the Massachusetts High Technology Council backed and campaigned successfully for Proposition 2½, a measure to roll back property taxes.

In 1951 the Council of Economic Advisers, chaired by Leon H. Keyserling, transmitted to President Harry S. Truman what was to become the post-war baseline report on the problems and opportunities of the New England economy. Though it found the burden of business taxes not to be as great as often believed, it also found there was widespread resentment against the level of taxes that often deterred business expansion. Consequently the Committee on New England, which prepared the report, recommended that business taxes be reduced to dissuade businessmen from thinking they were being treated unfairly and to show that New England recognized the importance of industrial strength relative to competitive states. The state tax burden per capita in the region was actually somewhat lighter than in competitive states but the local tax burden, composed mostly of property taxes, was much heavier.

The 1951 *New England Economy* study found the basic problem to be that the tax structures of the region's states were detrimental to their own economic development. Such a negative tax structure acted as a drag on the location, production, and expansion of industry. The study included the results of a survey by the Federal Reserve Bank of Boston which found that manufacturers "believe that the burden of state and local taxes is the worst drawback to their competitive position in a New England location."[9]

Three decades later business perceptions had changed little. In a more recent study of business climates in 48 states, prepared by the national accounting firm of Alexander Grant and Company in cooperation with the Conference of State Manufacturers Associations, New England finished as the second lowest ranked

Table 1–3   National Business Climate Rankings of New England States

State	1979	1980	1981
Conn.	38	47	42
Maine	15	24	40
Mass.	37	38	41
N.H.	21	9	24
R.I.	34	43	46
Vt.	23	27	30

SOURCE: From data published in the first through third studies conducted by Alexander Grant and Company, *Manufacturing Business Climates of the Forty-Eight Contiguous States of America* (Chicago: Alexander Grant and Co., 1980, 1981, 1982).

region in the view of businessmen. Table 1–3 shows the six state rankings for the most recent three years, New Hampshire ranking first in the region for 1981 but slipping to 24th place nationally. The study evaluates 18 quantifiable factors organized in five categories, including state and local government fiscal policies.

Consistent with the prevailing business view of three decades, New England in 1981 was ranked next to last among the eight regions for the category described as state and local government–controlled factors, including taxes, change in taxes, expenditure, debt, and welfare expenditures. For example, Massachusetts was one of the only three states nationally that had taxes during the 1980 fiscal year in excess of $135 per $1,000 of personal income. For the three years ending 1980, Maine was one of the two states where taxes increased at a faster rate than income, though it should also be pointed out that Vermont was one of only four states which had a decrease of greater than 15 percent. Connecticut was one of the five states that increased expenditures by 25 percent or more compared to their revenues. Rhode Island and Massachusetts were two of the only three states with welfare expenditures in excess of $300 per capita; the 48-state average was $173.

The negative business attitude toward the state and local tax burden in New England does not necessarily mean they will move to states with lower taxes in the sunbelt. Nor does the overall tax burden of the region apply equally to each of its states. Recent studies have shown that tax differentials are not of controlling importance to business and industry in inter-regional decisions concerning location or expansion. However, *within a region,* a favorable tax climate can become a pivotal factor in business location decisions; this has been the case in recent years with New Hampshire acquiring more of its new corporations from Massachusetts than from any other state.

While the location decision for a corporation does not depend primarily on a state's tax and fiscal policies, an often-cited study by the Harris Bank of Chicago confirms that states which reduce their tax burden relative to other states can expect to experience above-average economic growth.[10] The study found little relationship between economic growth of personal income and state-local tax burdens during the period from 1969 to 1976. However, after allowing for a three-year time lag, the study found a strong relationship between economic growth and reductions in state-local tax burdens.

Taxes, though not the major factor, do have a significant impact on both industrial perceptions of the business climate and opportunities for growth in New England. In the present economic climate the tax factor is becoming an increasingly important influence on business and employment. At the same time, it should be recognized that perceptions often lag behind reality. Data Resources, Inc., of Boston, a nationally recognized economic forecasting firm, found that high tax rates in New England produced the loss of an estimated 30,000 manufacturing jobs from 1973 to 1980.[11] That fact probably accounts in some measure for recent negative business attitudes about the business climates in New England. Now, as a result of reductions of the last few years, the region is expected to lose only a projected 3,200 jobs between 1982 and 1985 because of taxes. The new reality is that New England's taxes are no longer significantly above national norms and when that fact is driven home to the business sector, it can be expected that perceptions will change.

Ironically, the Massachusetts High Technology Council, known for supporting tax cuts, early in 1982 urged "state government to increase its investment in higher education."[12] Massachusetts alone has 46 percent of public enrollments and 63 percent of private enrollments in New England's higher education. In announcing its position, the Council acknowledged "the importance of higher education to the knowledge-intensive economy of Massachusetts and the fact that state support of higher education is well below the national average." This development augurs well for the future of higher education in Massachusetts and the region.

Weighing State Priorities

The budget expenditures of state government probably tell more about its policies and priorities than any other document. Decisions on the amount and proportion of state funds to spend for services are far more revealing than volumes of public rhetoric. In New England, where state and local expenditures per capita are 11 percent above the U.S. average, a sharply diminished share of those tax revenues is allocated to public higher education. Despite the political rhetoric, the higher education priority has simply been low in recent years. However, it must be remembered that as late as 1967, three of every five students were enrolled in *private* colleges and universities. A dramatic shift took place during a period of only 15 years so that today one of every two college students in New England is enrolled in *public* institutions. Nevertheless, two thirds of all the expenditures to operate higher education in the region are spent by private institutions.

The financial plight of public higher education outweighs even that of public elementary and secondary schools in the region. Per-pupil expenditures for the public schools in the three southern states are at least 10 percent greater than the national average. The three northern states each fall below the national average, although New England overall spends more per public school pupil than does the United States as a whole. We have seen earlier, however, that New England appropriates 21 percent less than the national average per college student.

In the nation's first knowledge-intensive economy, public higher education is now counted on to play a major role in providing the trained manpower needed for high technology industry and sophisticated professional services. The region can no longer rely on private colleges and universities as heavily as it has in the past. The demand for educated manpower required in the growth fields of the 1980s and beyond requires training and numbers to which the full system of higher education will need to respond. In addition, graduates of state and regional public and private colleges and universities are more likely than their counterparts in national private institutions to work and live in the region.

Government decision-makers must reassess the worth and contribution that higher education makes to their state and regional economies. The words of Peter Drucker seem especially relevant to the New England region. He wrote, "Knowledge has become the central expenditure and investment of a modern economy. Knowledge has become the economy's central resource."[13] In New England, the public sector of higher education and the private sector to a lesser degree have been acutely underfunded by government, which has been favoring other priorities. The question is whether those other priorities have the potential to contribute as much to a knowledge-intensive economy as higher education.

The changed condition of higher education need not produce crisis. Rapid economic change provides the opportunity to respond with vision and imagination to new responsibilities. Priorities can be shifted, programs restructured, and missions made clearer and more relevant to the needs of the economy, society, and the citizen. Given the huge resources already invested in higher education and those needed for a more productive future, it is reasonable to expect that shortcomings be overcome. Government must be supplied with better data by academia if it is to judge the effectiveness with which higher education uses the tax resources it receives. Government has the responsibility of providing the resources, but higher education must demonstrate it is using them productively for mutually approved objectives.

Endnotes

1. Marilyn McCoy and D. Kent Halstead, *Higher Education Financing in the Fifty States: Interstate Comparisons Fiscal Year 1976* (Washington, D.C.: National Institute of Education, 1979). D. Kent Halstead, "How States Compare in Financial Support of Higher Education 1981–82," (Washington, D.C.: National Institute of Education, February 11, 1982).
2. See Ward Curran's chapter, "Higher Education in the Gross Domestic Product of the New England States."
3. Estimated from preliminary data of the National Center for Education Statistics on "Current Funds Revenues and Expenditures for Colleges and Universities" (Bulletin, U.S. Department of Education, December 1981).
4. The figures on physical plant, endowments, and federal contracts and grants are for the most recent published year, *Financial Statistics of Institutions of Higher Education: Fiscal Year 1979* (Washington, D.C.: National Center for Education Statistics, 1981).
5. This data comes from unpublished material developed by the National Institute of Education and the National Center for Higher Education Management Systems, 1981.
6. Massachusetts Division of Employment Security, "High Technology Employment in Massachusetts and Selected States" (Boston, March 1981), p. 13.

7. Dan Dimancescu of the Technology and Strategy Group in Cambridge drew my attention to the public investment North Carolina is making in linking university research and development with technological innovation. He is co-author of the forthcoming book *Global Stakes* to be published by Ballinger Publishing Company in Cambridge, Mass., in the fall of 1982.

8. Lynn E. Browne, "How Much Government Is Too Much," *New England Economic Review*, March/April 1981, p. 25.

9. Committee on the New England Economy, *The New England Economy: A Report to the President* (July 1951), p. 119.

10. R. Genetski and Y. Chin, "The Impact of State and Local Taxes on Economic Growth" (Chicago: Harris Economic Research Office, 1978).

11. *Wall Street Journal*, March 4, 1982, p. 56.

12. Conference on Engineering Education, "MHTC Position on University/Industrial Relation," Hilton Inn, Natick, Massachusetts, February 10, 1982.

13. Peter Drucker, *Age of Discontinuity* (New York: Harper and Row, 1969), pp. 151–152.

Chapter 2

HIGHER EDUCATION: INVESTMENT OR EXPENSE?

by Michael S. McPherson

This chapter examines the economic benefits that may or may not result from spending on higher education. The purpose of this analysis is to shed some light on the economic justification (or lack of it) for raising and spending tax funds at both the state and federal levels to support the activities of colleges and universities. Necessarily, given the scope of activities of higher education, what follows is basically an overview and is therefore somewhat limited both in addressing specific issues of policy and in making points about the New England region. However, it can be useful, I think, in putting issues in context and in forming judgments about some broad issues of policy. In the final section of the chapter, I draw some specific conclusions that bear more directly on the New England region.

I would like at the outset to clarify the perspective suggested by the title of this chapter. The question "Should the funding of higher education be viewed as an investment or an expense?" invites consideration of education in purely economic terms, perhaps carrying the tacit implication that any expenditure on education that doesn't pay for itself in terms of higher GNP is merely a form of expensive recreation. Such a narrow view of the value of education seems to have considerable support in the Reagan

Note: I am grateful to Roger Bolton, Albert O. Hirschman, and Joseph Kershaw for helpful comments. Parts of this chapter rely on my paper, "Value Conflicts in American Higher Education: A Survey," forthcoming in the *Journal of Higher Education*.

Administration, at least to judge from the congressional hearings surrounding the 1982 National Science Foundation budget. One gets the sense that any activity that lacks a direct and preferably immediate connection to "economic recovery" is ripe for curtailment, if not elimination. Since the path to economic recovery remains somewhat obscure, this posture can easily provide the excuse for arbitrary and short-sighted budget making. It is sad to picture anthropologists staying up nights trying to hypothesize linkages between their research efforts and the nation's economic output. Whether or not such linkages exist, they are surely neither the purpose nor the justification for our modest national support of anthropological research. The same kind of comment applies to some areas of research, such as pure mathematics, that have fared rather better in the latest round of budget cuts. It sometimes happens, often after a great span of time, that some result in pure mathematics proves by pure happenstance to be of enormous practical value. But such coincidences really ought to be viewed as happy accidents, rather than as the sole foundation for our commitment to these activities.

Of course, the Reagan Administration is not operating in a vacuum, and its policies and rhetoric reflect the anxiety about economic performance that now pervades our society. This concern is understandable, but it has, I think, reached almost the level of obsession, and it is causing us to lose perspective on both national and personal goals that are more important than greater material wealth. It does seem that something central is lost when students view their education simply as a ticket to a better job and let their future career prospects dominate even their selection of particular courses, or when the nation views the search for new knowledge only as a way of beating the Russians or the Japanese.

It is probable that this "bottom line" mentality is not even optimal from the standpoint of promoting long-run economic growth. The attempt to appraise every expenditure for its economic payoff and to calculate each use of resources at the margin for its best use can easily damage the health and disrupt the internal coherence of both the teaching and the research enterprises. I believe a strong case can be made that the kinds of fundamental discoveries we expect universities to produce, and the kinds of enlightenment we hope they will bring to students, can come about only in an atmosphere of open intellectual exploration, where truth, not "payout," is the proximate goal. To get practical payoffs from the university's efforts, we have to re-spect and support the pursuit of knowledge, and that means pro-viding support for activities and explorations that have no obvious economic purpose—or, indeed, that obviously have no economic purpose. An instructive analogy might be made here to recent arguments that the success of Japanese business management de-rives in part from a resistance to viewing its responsibilities in narrowly financial and economic terms, and instead taking a longer and wider view of the enterprise as a human and social entity.

This argument says that even if the ultimate purpose of sup-porting higher education is to foster economic growth, the best strategy for achieving that end may be a roundabout one which avoids scrutinizing every expenditure too closely for its investment return. Plainly, GNP growth is not the only social purpose to which higher education contributes. For one thing, GNP is itself an inadequate measure of welfare. Suppose, for example, an ad-vance in medical research enables us to prevent some dire disease. Then the output of the medical care sector—which of course measures only treatment of sick people—will fall, and moreover, the productivity of resources in the health care sector (as mea-sured) will show no tendency to rise. If education makes people better parents or better citizens, or even better teachers, our output and productivity measures will capture the effect at best only very indirectly, and most likely not at all, even though our society will clearly be better off.

Another limitation on GNP as a measure of welfare is that it assumes that another dollar of income accruing to a wealthy person adds as much to social welfare as does another dollar for a poor person, a value judgment that few thoughtful people really want to accept. The capacity of educational reform by itself to produce social equality was badly oversold in the 1960s, but it remains true that an important part of the justification for higher education expenditure (and especially federal expenditure) is to encourage "access" to higher education for children of lower income families, and thereby to contribute to greater equality.

But there is a point here that goes deeper than questions about the adequacy of particular welfare measures. Much work in the humanities and a good deal in the social sciences is concerned not with promoting our favored social values, but precisely with crit-icizing the values of our society and with keeping before our minds the fact that other standards of value and ways of living can exist

and have existed in the world. To cite one example: A good deal
of interesting work has been done recently by philosophers and
economists that criticizes the use of cost-benefit analysis as a standard for social decision-making. Such work is plainly valuable, but
surely it's a bit absurd to imagine evaluating support of it by cost-
benefit standards. A commitment to critical reason is needed to
make possible a fully meaningful affirmation of our beliefs and
values: We cannot genuinely trust what we may not examine and
question. And by safeguarding traditions of critical inquiry in any
area—politics, natural science, the humanities—we help to safe-
guard it in the others, by underscoring that the fundamental standards and criteria in the academic realm are as nearly independent
as may be from the currently prevailing assumptions in our society.
These activities deserve our support for reasons more basic than
economics.

The above must seem an odd beginning for a chapter on the
economic significance of higher education. It is the custom for
economists to bury their remarks about the limits of the economic
perspective in the footnotes, rather than to trumpet them in the
introduction. But it is precisely because the economic framework
can give such an appearance of solidity and precision that we need
to keep in mind what's left out. Obviously many individuals un-
dertake education with the goal in mind of improving their economic status.* And much social expenditure on both research and
teaching has among its goals that of improving economic performance. There is nothing wrong with these goals when they are
kept in proper perspective, and not made to seem the be-all and
end-all of education's role. It is in order to resist that dangerous
misinterpretation that I have begun as I have.

Education as an Economic Investment

Economists think of investment as the act of purchasing or producing a capital good, and capital goods are defined by two properties, their durability and their role in the production process.

---

*And always have. As Alfred North Whitehead wrote in 1929, "I do not believe
that the modern parent of any class is any more mercenary than his predecessors.
When classics was the road to advancement, classics was the popular subject
for study."[1]

A durable good such as a piece of machinery yields up its services over a span of time. This feature generates a fundamental problem in thinking about capital goods, namely the need to weigh an expenditure taken at one time (or over some period of time) with the value of services that are provided at a later time. Capital goods are also typically thought of as playing an intermediate role in production, being owned by firms to aid in the production of other goods, rather than by consumers for use in the home. Of course, some durable goods are used at home—the home itself being the prime example. Most economists would be inclined to view the purchase of such "consumer durables" as "investment" rather than "expense," since the fundamental problem of comparing present costs to future benefits arises for such goods. This also makes for more consistent accounting, for otherwise we have to say that when Hertz buys a car to lease to you, that's investment, but when you buy it to use for the same travel purposes, it's consumption.

The notion that education has the requisite characteristics of durability and productive value to define it as an investment has been around at least since Adam Smith, who cited "the skill, dexterity, and judgment" of the labor force as one of the two great determinants of "the wealth of nations." But serious pursuit of the idea that an educated labor force could profitably be viewed as a kind of "human capital" began only in the late 1950s. The "human capital" research program emerged from the attempt to understand the growth record of the wealthy nations of the West and to account for the gap between their wealth and the poverty of much of the rest of the world. One striking fact was that the sheer accumulation of the traditional factors of production (physical capital, land, and labor) was not nearly rapid enough to account statistically for the pace of growth in the United States and Europe; nor was the gap in physical capital enough to explain the income gap between rich and poor nations.

A basic part of the solution to this puzzle seemed to be that changes occurred in the course of development not only in the sheer *quantity* of inputs made available to production, but in their *quality* as well. The physical capital American workers possessed in 1950 was not only more than in 1900, it was better, as a result of technical change. And, as T. W. Schultz argued with great effectiveness, the workers themselves were better too, because they were healthier and better educated. They possessed skills and capacities which were durable and productive—in a word, human capital. Thus, rather abruptly, two sectors of the economy that had always been seen as major users of resources—health care (including public health) and education—came into focus as important sources of the productive power of industrial nations.[2] At the same time the search for the sources of the technical change which led to improvements in physical capital turned attention to the contributions of university-sponsored basic research to economic growth. It will be useful to consider in turn these two economic functions of the higher education sector—the production of education and training and the production of research.[3]

The Value of Education and Training

Only a small portion of the total fund of skills, knowledge, and personal attributes that make up the productive capacity of the work force can be directly attributed to higher education. Besides the substantial investment in elementary and secondary schooling, very substantial investments are made by parents in the care of their children and by workers and firms in the form of on-the-job training, both formal and informal. Separating out the magnitudes and productivity of these various forms of investment is very difficult, but there is little doubt that their aggregate size and effect is enormous. Indeed, Schultz and others have shown that the aggregate productive value of the work force is larger and has grown faster than the value of the capital equipment with which they work.[4]

Evidence for the economic value specifically of higher education is based largely on a huge number of studies that have compared the earnings of college and high school graduates and—after controlling for other relevant differences between the groups—have attributed the remaining differences to the productivity-enhancing effects of education.[5] As with most statistical work in the social sciences, there are important disagreements about how to interpret the results of these studies,[6] but the bulk of them show that for most of this century the financial return on a student's time and money invested in higher education has been on the order of 10 to 15 percent per year after adjusting for inflation—well above the return on other investments available to most people, even ignoring any "consumption" benefits people obtain from education. This picture changed somewhat in the 1970s, a point to which I will return.

These studies give us an idea of the value the market puts on possession of a college degree, but they don't provide much sense of what it is about the "educational transformation," as Marc Nerlove has termed it, that makes those who have undergone it more productive.[7] Here there seem to be several sides of the story worth pursuing.

Some part of post-secondary education is fairly straightforward vocational training—the acquisition of skills that are directly useful on the job. This is the case with many offerings of two-year colleges and with parts of the education of technical specialists, such as engineers, computer scientists, and chemists. The economic importance of such technical training has been underlined by the current shortages of some categories of engineers and especially of computer scientists. The extremely rapid spread of computer technologies and microelectronics has led to an explosion of demand for such personnel which, ironically, is made all the harder to fill because the teaching of engineering and computer science has become markedly less lucrative than practicing in those fields. Engineering is notoriously a field of alternating "booms" and "busts," and it is hard to predict how long the current shortage will last. However, a National Science Foundation–Department of Education report last year identified this shortage of technical personnel as a potential major bottleneck in expanding the capacity of the economy over the next decade—a bottleneck that will grow much tighter if the demands for technical personnel implicit in the Reagan defense budget come to be realized.[8]

The "Credentialist" View of Education

While the development of technical skills is obviously an important result of some higher education, it plainly cannot be the whole story. Most specific skills in nontechnical fields—and many within them—are learned on the job and not in formal schooling. Thus a bank hiring a typical Williams College graduate will rightly assume that the student learned essentially nothing immediately "useful" in college, and will start from scratch with a fairly elaborate management training program. Why, then, do employers who are not after specific job skills seek out and pay a premium for college graduates—and indeed for graduates of "good" colleges?

Part of the answer is that colleges perform a "screening" function: Because success in school is to some degree correlated to success on the job, employers will be inclined to prefer college graduates even if they've learned nothing of particular vocational value, simply because they have demonstrated a capacity to perform.[9] Differing versions of this "credentialist" view in fact underpin much criticism of the economic value of education. The argument says that even though the "sorting" of people by ability is of some social value, the race for educational credentials can easily become overextended, leading to resource waste and demoralization. Longer educational "ladders"—requiring college, say, for a job that used to require high school—may not much improve the sorting process but may add considerably to private and social costs. Higher education becomes a "defensive necessity," pursued not for its positive value, but to avert the drastic career prospects awaiting those without the right credentials.

This "credentialist" view raises important questions about the productivity-enhancing conception of education which cannot be readily dismissed. No one has yet devised a convincing empirical test for choosing between the "screening" and the "human capital" views of education. And no one who has spent much time in colleges can doubt that "screening" and "credentialing" are an important part of what goes on there, and that these concerns can easily override or subvert the educational concerns of both students and teachers. Still, it seems very unlikely that college is *only* a filter, simply because it is such an expensive one, both for students who must spend several years there and for the firms that pay a substantial premium to college graduates. If all college did for people who do not get vocational training was to sort them according to pre-existing abilities, it's hard to believe that the economy would not evolve cheaper screening methods, like tests and probation periods, to perform the same function.[10]

"Dealing with Disequilibria"—A Valuable Skill

Theodore Schultz has argued that the somewhat mysterious other thing that colleges do—besides providing vocational skills and credentials—is to increase students' ability to "deal with disequilibria," to respond flexibly and constructively to change.[11] Education, at least when it works well, makes people more independent-minded and resourceful, more able to communicate with and to learn from others. What is at stake here are very general intellectual and emotional capacities, rather than specific job skills. The cultivation of these capacities is perhaps more commonly associated with the ideal of liberal education, especially as articulated by philosophers like Whitehead and Dewey, but the economic importance of these attributes is well worth stressing as well.

The acquisition of these capacities is likely to be a much more durable investment than is mastery of specific job skills. In a rapidly changing economy, any specific skill is likely to become obsolete well within the span of an individual career. What is needed to be successful in the long run in the labor market is the capacity to adjust and to learn new skills as the technology changes.

In fact, as Schultz has argued, this "ability to deal with disequilibria" which makes education valuable may well be of use only in a rapidly changing society. In a technically and socially stagnant society where succeeding generations largely step into their parents' roles, most of what is needed can be readily learned by example and imitation. It is precisely because a society like ours is continually upsetting the applecart that the ability to learn, to respond to new situations in new ways, is valuable. Even economists, who perhaps thought they had things pretty well figured out in the 1960s, have discovered the importance of being able to learn new things.

These considerations suggest a cautionary point about what *kinds* of education are economically valuable. Both students, anxious to get a toehold in the labor market, and policy-makers, anxious to show quick and tangible returns on public expenditure, may overstress vocational training, which has value mainly in the short run, and underemphasize more general and liberal education, which may be a better long-run investment in economic well-being for both the individual and society. Since such a broader education is also the sort that people are more likely to desire "for its own sake" or for the sake of the noneconomic benefits it brings, it may well be that in a long-run view there is less of a sharp trade-off between an economically valuable and a "humanely" valuable education than we sometimes seem to think. For that matter, there is no clear way to draw the line between the economic and noneconomic benefits of such liberal learning. The capacity to reason well and to argue articulately may be as useful in a town meeting as in a board meeting, just as the ability to read with discrimination may be of value in cultural as well as professional pursuits. We lack measures of these "non-economic" benefits that are as clear-cut as the income differences we can observe between high school and college graduates, but there is no reason to think these benefits are unimportant, either to individuals or to society. Of course, it is not impossible to combine vocational and liberal components in a single curriculum. In fact, it seems likely that economic pressures on both colleges and students will lead to increasing experimentation with combining these features over the next decade.[12]

Can College Overeducate?

No discussion of the economic benefits of college education can ignore the labor market experience of the 1970s when, for the first time in decades, college students encountered serious difficulties landing good jobs. This downturn gave rise to books with titles like *The Overeducated American* and *The Case Against College*.[13] People graduating from college in the 1970s faced a triple whammy: They were graduating in unprecedented numbers, partly because they were the baby boom generation; the overall pace of economic growth had slowed; and, even worse, the relative growth of those parts of the economy that rely most on educated labor fell. As Richard Freeman has shown, the 1970s generation of college graduates has lost much of the advantage over high school graduates that previous generations possessed at the same point in their careers. The fall was especially marked for liberal arts and humanities graduates and for those with advanced degrees. The situation has improved somewhat from the trough of the early 1970s, but the market for college graduates in nontechnical fields remains weak.

It is not at all clear, however, that this downturn is a sign of long-run decline in the economic value of education. The relatively poor situation of 1970s graduates may not persist throughout their careers.[14] More important, there is a good likelihood that the market for college graduates will turn up by the late 1980s, as the "baby bust" years yield smaller numbers of graduates, and as the position of education-dependent sectors of the economy improves. Over the long run, it seems likely that education will be again, as it was in the past, a good investment for many individuals.

Risks and Benefits of Financing Higher Education

Part of the economic case for higher education is that it produces
social as well as purely personal benefits. For example, college
graduates are, on average, more politically active and more likely
to occupy positions of community leadership. These and similar
benefits, although hard to measure and value, may justify public
subsidies to encourage more people to attend college. The wider
extension of college enrollment also promotes equal opportunity.
These are both familiar and important, though still controversial,
rationales for public support of higher education. But there is
another reason more closely related to the value of higher education as a pecuniary investment, and which is therefore worth
discussing in more detail in the present context.

The productive capacity of an economic enterprise depends on
the amount and quality of the physical capital embodied in its
plant and equipment and the human capital embodied in its workers. From a policy point of view, a crucial difference between
these two categories of assets is that (at least in modern times)
we expect the firm to supply the physical capital which the workers
employ but, to a large degree, we expect workers to produce and
pay for their own human capital. This imposes a very significant
burden of financing and risk on the worker, who is somewhat in
the position that a secretary would be in if she were expected to
supply her own word processor as a condition of employment. A
college education is a very substantial asset, which can easily cost
over $100,000 in time and money.

A firm making that sort of investment in a piece of machinery
has several advantages over an individual student (and her family)
investing in education. First, the firm can finance the asset by
putting the asset itself up as collateral for a loan, giving it easier
access to the credit market. It's not terribly easy or profitable to
repossess a college education, so private lenders would prefer to
finance a house or a car rather than an education, in the absence
of some other collateral or guarantee. Second, a firm contem-
plating a risky investment has ways to spread that risk. Any particular venture of the firm will be averaged in with its overall
operations in determining its profitability, whereas for most individuals their "human capital" is essentially the only productive
asset they possess. Moreover, incorporated firms have the option
of financing investment through the stock market, promising inves-

tors a share in possible gains against the risk of a loss—a loss which for shareholders is limited to the amount of their investment. Students and families who do borrow to finance education must do so at fixed interest, so that they alone bear all the chances of extraordinary gain or loss.[15]

The Difficulties of Individual Investment

While college education pays off on the average, it is a fairly risky pecuniary investment for the individual, who is typically uncertain of his own abilities and career plans, let alone what future job markets will be like. The implication of all this is that in the absence of some kind of public intervention, private lenders and investors will be systematically biased in favor of physical capital and against human capital investments. The result will tend to be underinvestment in education and slower economic growth than could be obtained by shifting the same total amount of investment funds toward human investment. The underinvestment will tend to be particularly severe among poorer families, who lack the ability to self-finance or to borrow against other collateral.

These difficulties in the private financing of higher education provide an important part of the economic rationale for public support of higher education, quite apart from arguments about equal opportunity or social benefits. One could argue that an ideal scheme focused purely on overcoming these financing difficulties need involve only devices to correct the loan market, so that family financing of education would be put on the same basis as business financing of physical investments, with no direct subsidies to students or schools. Such an idealized scheme would be based on government guaranteed loans at competitive interest rates, but with very long payback periods—say thirty or forty years to match the period over which the benefits of education accrue—and some sort of insurance provision to reduce the amount that must be paid back by those who wind up with low incomes because their educational investments haven't worked out.[16] (One way to arrange such insurance would be to require borrowers to pay back a fixed percentage of their income above a certain level, rather than a fixed amount of money, so that those whose investments didn't "pay off" would face a smaller obligation.) This second provision would be comparable to risk-sharing arrangements that are available on physical capital investment. It is arguable whether such an idealized scheme would be at all feasible or practical, and whether, if it were, there would not still be compelling reasons of other kinds to subsidize schools and students. It is interesting to note that the existing patchwork of arrangements for financing higher education actually has a number of the features that would be desirable in a scheme to encourage optimal investment in human capital.

Most obvious is the availability of government-guaranteed loans at the federal level and from some states. These provide access to the loan market on attractive terms for students and, in states with parent loan programs, for their families. Analysis is complicated by the fact that the loans are not only guaranteed, but also contain an interest subsidy which, because of current high interest rates, is much larger than was probably ever intended. Some subsidy could probably be justified as a "second best" means of compensation for the risk of human capital investment, but the recent cutback in the interest subsidy certainly makes sense. It is also reasonable to exclude high income families, who have good access to private credit markets, from the program. But it is not so clear that the recent decision to limit borrowing by "upper-middle" income families (those in roughly the $30,000 to $75,000 income range) to the extent of "need" makes as much sense, since it may be difficult for many of these families either to finance the so-called "parental contribution" out of current income, or to borrow on reasonable terms without a loan guarantee. A good deal can be said for allowing students and families to borrow a certain amount of money at a subsidized rate, and more at a higher rate, but still with a government guarantee. This, in effect, is what the parent loan program does in states that offer it. There is also an argument for extending substantially the repayment period on student loans to better match the period over which the return on the investment is realized.

Another attractive feature of the present financing system is that in some aspects it favors low income people over those with higher incomes. This is obviously desirable in terms of the social goal of fostering equal opportunity, but it is also justified on narrower investment grounds, since lower income people have less access to the loan market. The dramatic differences that existed not many years ago among different income, racial, and sexual groups in college attendance rates marked both a real injustice and a drastic waste of human resources. Federal and state grant systems, as well as the financial aid arrangements at most colleges, target aid at lower income students and families and have probably been important in reducing, though by no means eliminating, this gap.[17]

One of the less attractive features of the present financing system from an investment point of view is the substantial operating subsidy provided by state governments to public institutions to make up for the low tuitions in that sector. These subsidies may have the effect of distorting choices between public and private institutions and even among public institutions. Moreover, much of the operating subsidy may be poorly targeted from the standpoint of encouraging investment in education since it goes to reduce the costs for many students who would likely attend college anyway. There is a case for transferring state funds from operating subsidies to loan guarantee programs and to programs to subsidize further the education of lower income students.[18]

Nobody would defend the American higher education financing system as ideal, but it pretty clearly does work on balance to encourage worthwhile investments in education which would not be made without public support. In fact, calculations of the social returns to higher education, which compare estimates of the full social cost of college education to the benefits that result, suggest that higher education is a productive social investment, with real rates of return above 10 percent per year.[19] This is so even though such calculations typically ignore important classes of possible benefits of higher education, including non-money benefits to individuals and indirect social benefits such as improved citizenship.

The Impact of Budget Cuts

The cuts in the 1982 federal budget will probably not have a serious direct impact on the higher education system, although the pressures on state budgets which will result from reductions in federal support for a variety of state government functions may have an important indirect effect on state support for higher education. The coming decline in the college age population may also reduce the demand for the services of colleges and universities, and thus provide some room in higher education budgets, although costs will decline less rapidly than numbers. However, sustained budget cutting at both state and federal levels may well significantly reduce public support for higher education. And, indeed, it appears likely that the Reagan Administration will push for really big cuts in the federal higher education budget over the next few years, if it can get Congress to go along. One important rationale for such budget cutting is, in effect, to sustain a program of tax reductions aimed at stimulating business investment. This could easily prove to be a bad trade, even in strictly economic terms, especially since the budget cuts will not be perfectly targeted on "waste" in government spending for higher education, and future tax reductions like those in 1981 may be poorly designed to stimulate physical investment. To the extent that budget cuts are made which substantially discourage investment in education,* we could well lose more in human capital than we gain in physical capital. To cite a conjectural but telling example: Budget cuts at the state or federal level that would significantly retard growth in either the number or quality of engineers would likely be a bad trade against adding more equipment—and the new equipment would be less productive without enough qualified engineers to use it.

The Value of Basic Research

Instruction of students accounts for about two thirds of the expenditures of college and universities. Research efforts account for most of the rest, or about one quarter of the total expenditure, adding up to a national investment of well over $10 billion per year in university research.[20]

Advances in knowledge are a fundamental source of economic growth, with one well-known estimate crediting them with nearly a third of the increase in productivity of the American economy in the twentieth century.[21] Only a fraction of this new knowledge comes from formalized research efforts in the United States; the majority results from informal learning processes in industry and from research conducted abroad. Still, there is convincing evidence that the social returns on investment in research and development are high, with many estimates implying annual rates of return of 30 to 50 percent or more.[22] Moreover, estimates of

---

*There is some evidence that reductions in the "quality" of schooling (as measured by resources per student or by quality-ranking of school) impair the production value of the education received.

the contribution of research to productivity probably substantially understate its full value, because conventional output measures fail to register properly the value of new products and of improved product or service quality.

Despite the high returns, there are important barriers to private investment in research and development. These are partly due to the risky character of such investments, but, more importantly, they derive from the difficulty private firms have in capturing as profit the returns from an investment in research. Knowledge developed in one firm can often be readily learned by other firms, who thus benefit from the discovery without sharing the costs of the search. Patents and trade secrets limit this effect, but fundamental discoveries about how nature works, the products of so-called "basic" research, are very hard to patent or keep secret, nor would it be socially desirable for such discoveries to be held secretly by firms. As a result, less than 5 percent of industrial research and development expenditure goes for basic research— and that percentage has been dropping over the last two decades.*[23]

The American response to this difficulty has been to concentrate the basic research function in universities, which are not dominated by the profit motive, and to provide universities with substantial government funds to support their research efforts. Well over half of all basic research in the sciences is performed in academic settings. The chain of causation linking basic scientific discoveries in the university with specific industrial innovations is by no means easy to draw, but the reliance of the entire industrial research effort on a base of advancing scientific knowledge generated in universities seems reasonably evident. The ways in which advances in molecular biology have opened up the commercial field of genetic engineering, and in which the earlier advances in solid-state physics made microelectronics possible, illustrate the process. The intimate connection between graduate education and research is evident here, since industrial R&D staffs increasingly consist of people who have learned how to use the results of basic research by helping to carry out that research as graduate students.

---

*The recent tax bill provides incentives for basic research in industry. There is considerable doubt, however, that the incentives are large enough to have much impact. Whether it would even be desirable to shift a large proportion of the basic research effort from universities to industry is a large question. I am inclined to think not, but there is not space here to discuss the issue.

Government support of basic research began declining in real terms in the late 1960s and, despite some recovery in the late 1970s, it has still not returned to earlier levels. Since there is obviously a long lag between scientific discoveries and their commercial application, it is tempting to blame our current productivity problems on this decline in research funding. In that context Zvi Griliches' remark of 1973, that "we are unlikely to observe the effects of the current drought in research support very soon, but it may come back to plague us in the late seventies," has the ring of prescience.[24] The productivity problem, however, has complex roots, and the most careful studies suggest that reductions in research funding have not to date been an important cause of the productivity slowdown.[25] Still, it seems likely that research can play a quite significant role in economic recovery. Indeed, the fact that much of the slowdown may be due to the disruptive effects of higher energy prices points to at least one area where research efforts may be of unusual importance.

Measuring Economic Returns and Determining Research Priorities

No one has devised convincing ways of measuring the economic return on particular past investments in basic research, let alone predicting future returns, which are inherently uncertain. Thus we really have only a vague notion of whether current levels of public expenditure on basic research are adequate from an economic viewpoint. That industrial R&D continues to provide a return well above that on physical capital, and that such industrial R&D is dependent on basic research, are facts that provide good reason to believe we are at least not overspending on basic research.

The problem of determining research priorities among scientific fields is even more elusive.[26] The links connecting discoveries to applications are often surprising and indirect—as Harvey Brooks has noted, it is almost inconceivable that someone who set out at the beginning of the twentieth century to find a way to inspect the internal state of bodily organs would have been led to think up the X-ray. This uncertainty alone would be reason to grant the scientific community considerable autonomy in their choice of basic research projects, and to provide support even in areas where immediate payoffs aren't evident. It also seems likely that

drastic changes in funding levels, in reaction either to faddish
excitement or to disappointment, are counterproductive. The gush
of funds for the "war on cancer" undoubtedly led to considerable
waste as money went in search of proposals to fund, and it seems
likely that the spectacular increases in military R&D that are
proposed will have a similar effect. Similarly, the sudden cutoff
of social science funding will disrupt much research in progress
and may impair the continuity and momentum of a good deal of
social science research. The proposed cuts in the social science
budgets have been based on a claim that these subjects are less
relevant to economic performance than others, but this claim has
gone largely undefended. In fact, an important component of
federally funded social science research is focused explicitly on
economic goals. Examples include studies of worker motivation
and work organization, saving incentives, efficient health care
delivery, and macroeconomic forecasting. There does indeed seem
to be justification for Griliches' allegation that these selective social
science cuts were based on "vindictiveness, ignorance, and
arrogance."[27]

It is hard to make this kind of point against a "meat-axe" approach to science funding without falling into a kind of thoughtless
complacency. I share with many other economists a sense that
federal financing in our own discipline, and likely in others, has
a tendency to get stuck in a self-justifying rut, in which success
in past grant competitions lends scholars the authority to define
the criteria of success in future grant competitions, and so leads
to the perpetual pursuit of certain avenues of investigation and
the relative neglect of others. Occasional "shocks" to the funding
system may knock it out of the rut, and it is not inconceivable
that the current shake-up will have that unexpected result. At the
same time, it is hard to believe that drastic changes in overall
funding levels are at all close to the "optimal shock." A more
promising approach, if the aim were to stimulate fresh thought
in the social sciences, might be to divert a certain amount of the
financing out of the routine channels, and award it in a more
adventurous way, perhaps through panels of distinguished teachers who are nevertheless clearly out of the mainstream of the
usual grant-making machinery. Of course, there is bound to be
some tension between venturesomeness and accountability in the
use of public funds, but an occasional push against the boundaries
of routine may be both feasible and valuable.

The Plight of the "Elite" Research University

A central fact about academic research in science and engineering is that much of it is performed at a relatively small number of nationally known institutions. In 1977 just sixty institutions accounted for over two thirds of all the expenditures on university-based research and development in the United States.[28] These places play a vital role in the intellectual and economic life of the nation, and the issue of their health during the 1980s is worth stressing. The major research universities must make a variety of difficult adjustments in the 1980s. Because demographic trends imply that undergraduate enrollments are likely to be stable or to decrease over the decade, some departments at these schools will need to contract their graduate programs, and many will find it difficult to make room for new faculty. At the same time, physical equipment put in place during the great expansion of the 1960s is aging and in need of replacement. Sustaining an active and creative research environment in the face of these strains will not be easy. Furthermore, because these institutions perform national and even international functions, they often lack a powerful local constituency. Their "elite" quality may position them badly for intra-state competition for funds in the 1980s. The health of these institutions will thus be extremely dependent on their own internal resources and resourcefulness, and on the willingness of the federal government to continue its support of basic research.[29]

The Impact of Reaganomics

The Reagan Administration's intentions regarding research in universities are by no means clear. The most apparent trend is a massive shift of funds for "mission-oriented" research from domestic agencies like the Department of Health and Human Services to military-related spending in the Departments of Defense and Energy. Support for basic research in the National Science Foundation budget has survived Administration budget cut proposals essentially intact, with the notable exceptions of the drastic cutback in support for social science and the surprising elimination of the budget for science education. But in the absence of any coherent statements from the Administration about the rationale of these budgetary decisions, it is hard to read their meaning for the longer range prospects of science funding.

It is reasonable to speculate that there are actually two cross-cutting tendencies at work. On one hand, the Reagan Administration is philosophically committed to a program of fundamentally rebuilding the United States' technological and economic strength. Such a program needs a long time horizon, and suggests support for a strong program in basic research and science education, with relatively little concern for short-run payoff. On the other hand, the present Administration, like those of the recent past, also seems to want a "quick fix" for our economic troubles, preferably before the next election. This attitude points toward support for "safe" research investments, with quick and reliable returns. This stance will tend to pull the Administration away from longer term and riskier investments in fundamental research, and away from programs like science education in the elementary and secondary schools, whose results are a couple of elections away. The struggle between these tendencies, on the one hand toward fundamental investment and on the other toward "cashing in" for a quick return in the research budget and elsewhere, will carry important implications for the nation's economic future.

Implications for the New England Region

By any account, higher education has become a major "industry," using resources at a rate of well over $50 billion per year, of which more than $25 billion is provided by governments.[30] It is natural that taxpayers and users of the system will wonder what they get for their money, and will expect the answer partly in economic terms. And it seems clear that such an answer can be given: Both the research and teaching functions of the university do play a central role in modern economic life. In an aggregate sense, it is fairly safe to say that expenditures on higher education more than pay for themselves, so that the nation would be poorer, in a strictly financial sense, if somehow the American higher education establishment were to be shut down. In this broad sense, higher education should surely be counted more as "investment" than "expense."

This of course is no cause for complacency about the state of American higher education, which could no doubt stand improvement, in terms of both economic efficiency and educational quality. Analysis of the investment benefits of education does not provide a precise measure of which lines of activity in colleges and universities are most productive, or indeed whether small increases or decreases in overall levels of expenditure would be an economic improvement. Our economic knowledge is simply not that precise in regard to either higher education or most other spheres of economic life.

On the other hand, it is very doubtful that we would really want to base decisions about educational policy on detailed economic calculations, even if we had the knowledge to make them. It is reassuring in a general way to know that much of our expenditure on education has an economic "pay-off," and no doubt we would view both teaching and research quite differently if we had reason to believe that no economic benefits flowed from them. Still, an educational system geared single-mindedly to the maximization of economic benefits would be radically distorted from a social and educational point of view. I suspect very few of us would want for our own children an education whose aims and orientation were mainly economic. Nor would I or many others want to teach at a university that evaluated and supported research according to its market value.

That being said, it remains important to see what implications this general analysis of the economic value of higher education carries for current policy discussions about higher education in the New England economy. I should like in this concluding section to spell out three such points, at least a couple of which cut against some conventional thinking about the role of higher education in regional development, and which may therefore be of special interest. It would be pushing things to say that these conclusions "follow" from the discussion so far, since they reflect my own values and perspective on the issues. But they are, I think, consistent with the preceding analysis.

New England's Interest in a National Financial Aid Policy

Federal policy has become increasingly important in shaping both the scope and the character of American higher education, accounting by now for roughly a quarter of national expenditures at colleges and universities.[31] Since New England is disproportionately important both as a producer of higher education and as a user of highly educated labor and of research results, the region has a strong interest in a sane and supportive federal policy toward higher education in the 1980s. Effective articulation of this interest in national policy forums may be as important as anything that can be done locally. Two areas to single out are financial aid policy and support for basic research in universities.

A strong case can be made on the grounds of both equity and efficiency for the federal government to continue to play a major role in helping students from lower income families to finance their college educations. Some erosion of this part of the federal financial aid commitment occurred in the 1970s, as budgetary increases have more and more often gone toward loan subsidies that tend to benefit middle and upper income students and toward extending into higher reaches of the income distribution eligibility for basic grant aid (formerly BEOGs; now called Pell grants). Meanwhile, the maximum award under the Pell grant program, which sets the ceiling on what the poorest student can receive, has not nearly kept up with inflation or rising college costs; it is now worth perhaps two thirds of what it was when the program was introduced in the early 1970s. It is possible to support the Administration's efforts to tighten eligibility for Pell grants and to restrict the loan program while still trying to ensure at a minimum that help for the neediest students is not eroded further. A recent proposal from the Office of Management and Budget calls for cutting the budget for Pell grants and the campus-based aid programs from $4.2 billion to $1.4 billion by 1984, a cut which would be certain to devastate the programs. These programs are by now a quite significant source of revenue for New England's colleges and universities. More important, they provide essential financial support to many of the region's students. In 1979–1980, for example, dependent students from families with incomes below $18,000 received more than half their total support from federal student aid programs.[32] In the mid-1970s basic grants paid 30 percent of the cost of black students' higher education.[33] To lose these groups from its student population would be a serious blow to New England higher education and society.

Two particularly bad ideas might appear on the federal financial aid policy agenda in the next few years and should be guarded against. One would be proposals to shift federal aid responsibilities to the states, in line with the "new federalism." This is unattractive not only because the states don't have the revenues to do this job and because the commitment to equal opportunity is fundamentally a national commitment, but also because high levels of cross-state migration of students make the states inappropriate units for financing such programs on a large scale. The other danger is that the idea of a tuition tax credit for colleges and universities will be resurrected, probably on the coattails of such a credit at lower education levels. Although there is room for reasonable debate about the worth of such a credit at elementary and secondary levels of education, there is close to universal agreement among economists, observers of higher education, and members of the higher education community that such credits for college would be wasteful, ineffective, and inequitable. Still, they have come close to passage before, and in the current climate they may, if the proposal resurfaces, have a better chance than ever before.

Concerning federal research funding, I stressed earlier the national importance of the major research universities, and the special difficulties they will face in the 1980s. New England has more than its share of such universities, and the immediately surrounding parts of the Northeast have more. While the states and the region certainly derive important benefits from these institutions and have at least a responsibility to avoid policies that would do them unnecessary harm, such as the occasional moves to remove the tax exemptions from which private institutions benefit, it is clear that the major public responsibility for the health of these places is a national one. Capricious swings in federal research support—either in levels or in distribution across fields—could prove quite damaging, and New England's leaders should be outspoken in resisting them. Business financing of university research is, of course, on the upswing; but its absolute amount remains small, and it could in no way make up for substantial cuts in federal support.

I might add here a sceptical note about the use of special federal tax incentives, beyond the usual deductibility of charitable gifts, to encourage either basic research in industry or industrial support for university research. Public finance economists are usually negative about such "tax expenditures" because they are hard to monitor and control and because it is extremely difficult to design them artfully enough to elicit the desired behavior. Consider, for example, the problems defining "basic research" in industry and in trying to ensure that a tax credit goes mainly to stimulate added basic research, rather than rewarding what would be performed anyway. Although any particular proposal should of course be

looked at on its merits, there is a general presumption in favor
of the government appropriating funds directly to support whatever research activities are deemed worthwhile, and to support
them at whatever location seems likely to do the best job.

The Independence of Higher Education

A sense of urgency about the need for universities and colleges
in the region to contribute to the economic development of New
England can easily lead to a measure of resentment at what is
seen as their "aloofness" or at what John Hoy has called "the
traditional stance of observational reserve and detached analysis
which has been the privileged role of the higher education community."[34] I can readily enough sympathize with his desire to get
us academics down from our ivory towers and to face up to our
role as citizens of the region. But some of what may be thought
of as "aloofness" could also be styled "independence," and the
analysis above underlines the value of that independence.

A noneconomic point should perhaps be made first, that members of universities perform a valuable social function as critics
of prevailing beliefs and values, including the role as critics of
particular strategies of economic development or even of the value
of such development itself. Nobody, least of all John Hoy, wants
to undermine that sort of independence, but I think it is clear
that a certain degree of academic detachment from particular social
goals and causes is important to preservation of that independence.
To raise a related issue: If we encourage too strongly the trend
for university scientists to be intimately involved in the commercial exploitation of the discoveries they make, we may find
ourselves in the awkward position of having no experts on significant technological developments who do not have a commercial
interest in their exploitation. I offer these points not in some
quixotic hope that universities should return somehow to an
imagined past state of virginity, but to caution against too one-
sided a view of the relation of the university to society.

But economic considerations also suggest that some university
functions are best performed at arms-length from particular social
needs. There is certainly a place, and perhaps a growing one, in
the academic environment for extension service, consulting, and
other attempts to bridge the gap between "abstract" knowledge
and practical problems. But it seems that universities are really

better designed for the most part as places to turn up interesting
leads or to make discoveries without *immediate* attention to their
practical results, rather than as resources for the solution of well-
defined problems. Both functions are important, but it may often
be best to look to other kinds of institutions—corporations, research institutes which may be "spun off" from universities—for
the latter. We certainly don't want universities to become preoc-
cupied with short-run "applied research and development" issues
to a degree that constrains their capacity to come up with the
fundamental new ideas that may be most significant in the long
run.

Something similar may be true on the teaching or "training"
side as well. As I argued earlier, strictly vocational training may
be a relatively small component of the increased value education
provides to workers. The more general capacities fostered by
higher education—independent thought, ability to communicate
effectively—may develop best in an environment that preserves
a degree of detachment from the flux of events. The question is
of course one of degree: What we are after is the elusive optimal
mix between "relevance" and "detachment."

This last point may have special relevance for some parts of
public higher education in the New England states over the next
decade. As excess capacity emerges in New England higher education, there may well be a tendency toward increased specialization of function among colleges and universities: In many ways
this would be desirable. This development, coupled with continued strong pressure from students for job-relevant education—
and an increasing desire among enrollment-hungry institutions to
give students what they want—is likely to make vocational training
an increasing part of the offering at many "lesser" public institutions. The same forces may affect a number of the less prestigious
private institutions as well. I see this as basically a healthy development, and one of potential benefit to New England industry.

The lurking danger in education that is too narrowly vocational
is precisely that its benefits won't last beyond the first change of
jobs, or the next important change in technology. It is important
in vocational training as in other education to develop students'
capacities to learn and to adapt, as well as to master specific skills.
In this sense some traditional elements of "liberal education"—
although perhaps not always taught in traditional form—deserve
a place in vocational curricula. An awareness of this need is not

likely to come from the students, whose attention is heavily focused on that first job; so it should come from educators and
policy-makers, who ought to be the ones to take a longer view.

Levels of Public Support for Higher Education

Many issues surround the levels of public support for higher education in New England, and are in fact the subject of the next
chapter. Here I would like simply to advance the proposition that
the low levels of public support for higher education in the region,
which are often cited with dismay, may well prove in the 1980s
to be a blessing in disguise.

The New England states typically spend about one half to two
thirds as large a percentage of their tax dollars on higher education
as does the nation as a whole, largely because public higher education is less extensive in the region than it is elsewhere in the
nation. Two hopeful possibilities are raised by this fact, in light
of the enrollment and fiscal difficulties we can anticipate. First,
the lower expenditures suggest that the public higher education
systems in these states are somewhat less overbuilt, relative to
the lower enrollment levels of the 1980s, than those of some other
states. This may counterbalance in some measure the likelihood
that the enrollment decline will be somewhat larger in New England than other regions, owing to a considerably sharper fall in
the college-age population. Much of the enrollment decline will,
of course, be felt by private institutions in the region, and they
will not find it pleasant. But I suspect that there is more chance
of getting a rational pattern of campus closings and retrenchments
from private institutions than from public institutions in conditions
of decline, because patterns of political pressures, while not ab-
sent, will be more muted.

Second, the relatively smaller state higher education budgets
may prove a less tempting target to state legislators responding
to fiscal pressures than larger budgets elsewhere in the nation.
New England state higher education budgets have so far escaped
the drastic cuts and threats of cuts that several states in other
regions have experienced. Thus, with luck and an effective presence in the state legislatures, New England may have a relatively
better chance of sustaining its smaller base of support during the
next decade than some states with more prominent but much
more expensive programs.

The real challenge for the decade, in this respect, will be to work out a genuinely viable relationship and desirable division of labor between public and private higher education in the region. The smaller scope of the public sector in the region provides an attractive starting point for doing that. It is hard, for example, to see how some of the midwestern states with much smaller though still significant private sectors will be able to work out desirable policies to encourage their survival. To do this will require finding the political discipline to ensure that public institutions take their share of whatever enrollment declines materialize, and to resist dissipating public funds in efforts to "bail out" failing institutions, whether public or private. The threat of excess capacity also provides an additional argument for moving state support away from institutional funding and more toward student aid, even at the expense of higher tuition in public institutions. Should New England succeed in preserving the exceptional quality and variety of the region's higher education, it will once again assert its role as a leader in national higher education.

Endnotes

1. A. N. Whitehead, *The Aims of Education and Other Essays* (New York: The Free Press, 1929), p. 62.
2. The groundwork for human capital economics was laid down in T. W. Schultz, "Optimal Investment in Human Capital," *American Economic Review* 51 (March 1961), pp. 1–17; T. W. Schultz, *The Economic Value of Education* (New York: Columbia University Press, 1963); Jacob Mincer, "Investment in Human Capital and Personal Income Distribution," *Journal of Political Economy* 66 (August 1958), pp. 281–302; and Gary S. Becker, *Human Capital: A Theoretical and Empirical Analysis, with Special Reference to Education* (New York: National Bureau of Economic Research, 1964).
3. See G. K. Douglass, "Economic Returns on Investments in Higher Education," chapter 12 of *Investment in Learning: The Individual and Social Value of American Higher Education* (San Francisco: Jossey-Bass Publishers, 1977).
4. Schultz, 1961, 1963, *op. cit.*; Edward F. Denison, *The Sources of Economic Growth in the United States and the Alternatives Before Us*, Supplementary Paper 13 (New York: Committee for Economic Development, 1962); and Edward F. Denison, *Accounting for Slower Economic Growth: the United States in the 1970s* (Washington, D.C.: The Brookings Institution, 1979).
5. Surveys of this literature include Douglass, 1977, *op. cit.*; Mark Blaug, "The Empirical Status of Human Capital Theory: A Slightly Jaundiced Survey," *Journal of Economic Literature* (September 1976), pp. 827–55; Sherwin

Rosen, "Human Capital: a Survey of Empirical Research," in *Research in Labor Economics: an Annual Compilation of Research*, R. G. Ehrenberg, ed. (Greenwich: JAI Press, 1977, vol. 1), pp. 3–40; and Carnegie Council on Policy Studies in Higher Education, *Three Thousand Futures: The Next Twenty Years for Higher Education* (San Francisco: Jossey-Bass Publishers, 1980), Supplement C.

6. In addition to the surveys mentioned in note 4, see P. Clecak, "Views of Social Critics," in *Investment in Learning: The Individual and Social Value of American Higher Education* (San Francisco: Jossey-Bass Publishers, 1977); C. Jencks, et al., *Inequality: A Reassessment of the Effect of Family and Schooling in America* (New York: Basic Books, Inc., 1972); and Mark Granovetter, "Toward a Sociological Theory of Income Differences," in *Sociological Perspectives on the Labor Market*, Ivar Berg, ed. (New York: Academic Press, 1981).

7. Marc Nerlove, "On Tuition and the Costs of Higher Education: Prolegomena to a Conceptual Framework," *Journal of Political Economy* 80 (May/June 1972, Supplement), pp. 178–218.

8. National Science Foundation and Department of Education, *Science and Engineering Education for the 1980s and Beyond* (Washington, D.C.: U.S. Government Printing Office, 1980).

9. Kenneth J. Arrow, "Higher Education as a Filter," *Journal of Public Economics*, 1973, pp. 193–216; A. Michael Spence, *Market Signaling: Informational Transfer in Hiring and Related Screening Processes* (Cambridge, Mass.: Harvard University Press, 1974); and J. E. Stiglitz, "The Theory of 'Screening,' Education, and the Distribution of Income," *American Economic Review*, June 1975, pp. 283–300. A variation on the screening view is Thurow's "job competition" model found in L. C. Thurow, *Generating Inequality: Mechanisms of Distribution in the U.S. Economy* (New York: Basic Books, Inc., 1975).

10. For a review of empirical tests of screening and elaboration on the point in the text, see John G. Riley, "Testing the Educational Screening Hypothesis," *Journal of Political Economy* 87 (October 1979, Supplement), pp. S227–S252.

11. T. W. Schultz, "The Value of the Ability to Deal with Disequilibria," *Journal of Economic Literature*, September 1975, pp. 827–43. From this perspective, some of the radical criticism of education can be understood as complaining that education too often does not aim to produce these qualities, because it prepares people for jobs that do not require them. See S. Bowles and H. Gintis, *Schooling in Capitalist America: Educational Reform and the Contradictions of Economic Life* (New York: Basic Books, Inc., 1976).

12. See E. F. Cheit, *The Useful Arts and the Liberal Tradition* (New York: McGraw Hill, 1975) and Clecak, 1977, *op. cit.*, for appraisal of proposals on these lines. A related notion is considered in James D. Koerner, ed., *The New Liberal Arts: an Exchange of Views*, an Occasional Paper from the Sloan Foundation (New York: Alfred P. Sloan Foundation, 1981).

13. C. Bird, *The Case Against College*, H. Mandelbaum, ed. (New York: Bantam Books, 1975); and Richard B. Freeman, *The Overeducated American* (New York: Academic Press, 1976). Freeman's work is updated in his 1981 paper,

"Implications of the Changing U.S. Labor Market for Higher Education," NBER Working Paper Series (New York: National Bureau of Economic Research, 1981).

14. This is argued in J. P. Smith and F. Welch, "The Overeducated American: A Review Article," unpublished, 1978.

15. A good discussion of these points is in Nerlove, 1972, *op. cit.*

16. See Marc Nerlove, "Some Problems in the Use of Income-contingent Loans for the Finance of Higher Education," *Journal of Political Economy* 83 (February 1975), pp. 157–83 and D. Bruce Johnstone, with the assistance of Stephen P. Dresch, *New Patterns for College Lending: Income Contingent Loans*, Ford Foundation Report (New York: Columbia University Press, 1972).

17. The reduction in the influence of income and race on likelihood of college attendance is documented in Carnegie Council, 1980, *op. cit.* There are still very important differences in the *kinds* of institutions (e.g., two-year versus four-year) attended by different income groups and in *lengths* of attendance.

18. For similar arguments, see Roger Bolton, "Higher Education for Everybody: Who Pays?" in W. Todd Furniss, ed., *Higher Education for Everybody?* 3 (Washington, D.C.: American Council on Education, 1971), pp. 185–201; D. W. Breneman, and C. E. Finn, Jr., "An Agenda for the Eighties," *Public Policy and Private Higher Education* (Washington, D.C.: The Brookings Institution, 1978), pp. 411–50; W. L. Hansen, and B. A. Weisbrod, "A New Approach to Higher Education Finance," in M. D. Orvig, ed., *Financing Higher Education: Alternatives for the Federal Government* (Iowa City: American College Testing Program, 1971), pp. 117–42; and T. W. Schultz, "Optimal Investment in College Instruction: Equity and Efficiency," *Journal of Political Economy*, May/June 1972, pp. 520–30.

19. See the surveys mentioned in note 5.

20. National Center for Education Statistics, *The Condition of Education: 1980 Edition* (Washington, D.C.: U.S. Government Printing Office, 1980).

21. Denison, 1962, *op. cit.*; and Edwin Mansfield, "Technology and Productivity in the United States," in *The American Economy in Transition,* Martin Feldstein, ed., National Bureau of Economic Research (Chicago: University of Chicago Press, 1980).

22. Zvi Griliches, "Issues in Assessing the Contribution of Research and Development to Productivity Growth," *The Bell Journal of Economics,* Spring 1979, pp. 92–115; Zvi Griliches, "Research Expenditures and Growth Accounting," in *Science and Technology in Economic Growth,* B. R. Williams, ed. (New York: Wiley, 1973); and Mansfield, 1980, *op. cit.*

23. Mansfield, 1980, *op. cit.* The basic arguments about public and private benefits of investments in research were made by Richard R. Nelson, "The Simple Economics of Basic Scientific Research," *Journal of Political Economy* 66 (June 1959), pp. 297–306; and Kenneth J. Arrow, "Economic Welfare and the Allocation of Resources for Invention," in *The Rate and Direction of Inventive Activity: Economic and Social Factors,* National Bureau of Economic Research (Princeton, N.J.: Princeton University Press, 1962), pp. 609–25.

24. Griliches, 1973, *op. cit.*, p. 61.

25. Zvi Griliches, "Research and Development and the Productivity Slowdown," *The American Economic Review,* May 1980, pp. 343–47; Denison, 1979, *op. cit.;* and Edward F. Denison, "Discussion," *The American Economics Review,* May 1980, pp. 354–55.

26. A valuable discussion is H. Brooks, "The Problem of Research Priorities," *Daedalus,* Spring 1978, pp. 171–89.

27. Zvi Griliches, "Foreclosing on the Future," *Transaction/Society* 18 (September/October 1981), p. 14. See also the articles in the same issue of *Transaction/Society* (September/October 1981) by Prewitt, Larsen, Riecken, Klein, Glass, and Horowitz on "Social Science and the Reagan Administration."

28. Commission on Human Resources, *Research Excellence through the Year 2000. A Report with Recommendations of the Committee on Continuity in Academic Research Performance* (Washington D.C.: National Research Council–National Academy of Sciences, 1979).

29. For further discussion of these issues, see CHR (1979) and B. L. R. Smith and J. J. Karlesky, *The State of Academic Science. The Universities in the Nation's Research Effort,* vols. I and II (New York: Change Magazine Press, vol. I 1977; vol. II 1978.)

30. NCES, 1980, *op. cit.*

31. Carnegie Council, 1980, *op. cit.*

32. David W. Breneman and Susan C. Nelson, *Financing Community Colleges: An Economic Perspective* (Washington, D.C.: Brookings Institution, 1981), p. 149.

33. Lorenzo Morris, *Elusive Equality: The Status of Black Americans in Higher Education* (Washington, D.C.: Howard University Press, 1979), p. 122.

34. John C. Hoy, "An Economic Context for Higher Education," in John C. Hoy and Melvin Bernstein, eds., *Business and Academia: Partners in New England's Economic Renewal* (Hanover, N.H.: University Press of New England, 1981), p. 25.

Chapter 3

FINANCE AND THE FUTURE OF HIGHER EDUCATION IN NEW ENGLAND

by Patricia Flynn Pannell

This chapter examines the financing of higher education in New England.[1] The regional institutional structure of higher education and its revenue and expenditure patterns are compared with the national norms. Within the region, distinctions in financing higher education are highlighted by state, institutional classification, and type of control.

The picture that emerges from this review is a region with a relatively high private sector orientation and a low level of state and local economic support for higher education, both in absolute and in relative terms. The low level of state and local support of higher education in New England, 30 percent below the national average in 1979, is not attributable to the particular mix of classifications of institutions in the region. Public funding is consistently below the national average for each institutional classification. Nor is it traceable to a lack of tax revenues in the region: Through 1979 (prior to Proposition 2½), state and local tax revenues collected per capita in the region exceeded the national average. The reason for the low level of public support, however, is clear: Higher education has a low budget priority.

This underfunding of higher education by state and local governments in the region occurs in both the public and the private

The author would like to thank Peter B. Doeringer and Jeremiah O'Connell for their helpful comments.

sectors. As a consequence, public institutions of higher education in New England, in each institutional classification, spend less on instruction, academic support, research, and public service than is true for public colleges and universities nationally. In contrast, the private sector procures enough revenue from tuition, private gifts and grants, and federal government contracts to generate spending levels on all aspects of educational services above the national average for private institutions.

Private colleges and universities in New England tend to spend significantly more per student than do their public sector counterparts. Public service expenditures provide the major exception, with the region's public institutions of higher education spending more than twice the amount (per capita) on public service than the private institutions.

The New England regional figures mask significant interstate diversity. Massachusetts, for instance, is a state with almost 60 percent of its enrollments in higher education in the private sector. Private sector instructional expenditures per student exceed those in public institutions by two thirds. Private sector research expenditures per faculty member are seven times higher than those in the public sector. Institutional revenues generated by tuition in the public institutions in Massachusetts are very low compared to regional and national figures.

Vermont presents a marked contrast to Massachusetts. The majority (55 percent) of the enrollments in higher education are in the public sector. Instructional expenditures per student are 50 percent higher in the public sector than in the private sector. In addition, public institutions spend over 30 times more on research per faculty member and almost 100 times more for public service than do private institutions. Tuition revenues per student in the public sector in Vermont are unusually high relative to the regional and national averages.

The next section presents a brief overview of higher education in New England. Succeeding sections focus on state and local funding patterns of higher education in the region, differences among the various institutional financing arrangements, and, finally, policy implications regarding the future financing of higher education in New England.

Overview of Higher Education in New England

Over 250 institutions of higher education are located in New England.[2] (See Appendix, Table 3A–1.) Traditionally, the region has maintained a much greater private sector orientation than is common in the United States overall. In 1979, two thirds of the region's colleges and universities were private, compared to just over half for the country as a whole.[3] Similarly, the proportion of private sector enrollments in New England was double that for the nation. (See Table 3–1.)

The enrollment mix within the region varies widely between public and private institutions. Massachusetts has the highest proportion of private sector enrollments, 59 percent, followed by Rhode Island with 52 percent. In Maine, Connecticut, New Hampshire, and Vermont the majority of the enrollments are in public institutions.

Massachusetts alone accounts for over half of New England's enrollments in higher education. Connecticut ranks second with one fifth of the enrollments, while each of the remaining four states accounts for between 5 and 10 percent of the region's students.

Four of the New England states (Massachusetts, New Hampshire, Rhode Island and Vermont) are net importers of students to higher education.[4] In 1979 in New Hampshire and Vermont, students from out of state accounted for over 40 percent of new enrollments. The majority of students migrating to the New England states for higher education attend private institutions, whereas New England residents who remain in their state for higher education tend to enroll in public institutions.

State Support of Higher Education

To place in perspective the financing of higher education in New England, it is important to view historically the roles of the states and the federal government in the support of higher education in the United States.

Table 3–1 Distribution of Enrollments* in Higher Education in New England, by Institutional Classification and by State, in 1979

	Conn.	Maine	Mass.	N.H.	R.I.	Vt.	N.E.	U.S.
Public Sector								
Universities	17%	30%	7%	30%	23%	36%	15%	24%
Professional and specialized	†	14	2	8	0	0	3	2
Other 4-year colleges	21	21	18	8	12	15	17	23
2-year colleges	21	5	13	9	14	5	14	27
Total, public colleges and universities	59%	70%	40%	55%	49%	56%	49%	76%
Private Sector								
Universities	9	0	31	12	14	0	21	6
Professional and specialized	1	8	8	12	20	6	8	13
Other 4-year colleges	29	20	16	19	17	35	20	2
2-year colleges	2	3	5	3	1	4	3	3
Total, private colleges and universities	41%	31%	60%	46%	52%	45%	52%	24%

NOTE: Totals for public and private institutions may not equal 100 percent due to rounding.
* Full time equivalents.
† Less than 1%.

Federal and State Roles in the Support of Higher Education

Constitutionally, under the 10th Amendment, the states bear primary responsibility for education at every level. From 1929 to 1980, however, the federal government played an expanding role in higher education in terms of both financial resources and the scope of policy intervention. As educational costs rose dramatically during those 50 years, there was a major shift from private to public sources of support. The federal government picked up much of the tab, increasing its share of public support to higher education from 9 percent in 1929 to 45 percent by the mid-1970s.[5]

Financing of higher education at the federal level tends to differ in form and objective from that of states. Unlike state aid, which tends to be "enrollment driven," federal aid has been "issue-oriented." For instance, the Service Readjustment Act of 1944 (the G.I. Bill), which funnelled millions of dollars into higher education, was enacted to assist servicemen in their integration into civilian life and to mitigate the impact of over ten million military personnel returning to the civilian labor market.[6] Sputnik and "national security" concerns resulted in the passage of the National Defense Education Act of 1958, which provided fellowships and loans to students in higher education. A shift in focus away from "meritocracy" toward "egalitarianism" occurred under the Higher Education Act of 1965.[7] Under this Act, federal monies supported programs designed to provide equal access to educational opportunities.

As the role of the federal government in aiding higher education evolved, the states continued to be the primary "guardian" of the system. That is, the states, through varied levels of commitment, continued to provide institutional support and were responsible for planning and coordinating the higher education system around the federally established priorities.[8]

Federal support has often taken the form of student aid as opposed to institutional aid. In contrast, little, if any, of state and local appropriations go to student aid—4 percent in 1979. Whereas federally funded student aid tends to follow the student to a public *or* private institution, the vast majority of state aid is earmarked specifically for public sector institutions. Half of the New England states (Maine, New Hampshire, and Vermont) restrict their institutional aid to the public sector; the remaining three states

appropriate state and local dollars to private institutions but at
rates well below the national average.

The allocation of institutional aid, much more than student aid,
brings to the forefront the issue of whether or not public funds
should be appropriated to the private sector. While the courts are
handling this question on a case-by-case basis, decisions to date
have held that the federal constitution generally does not prohibit
public funds from being allocated to private institutions, including
those that are religiously affiliated.[9] State constitutions, however,
may hinder or prohibit state aid to private higher education. In
addition to constitutional issues, philosophical questions regarding
matters of equal access, freedom of choice, accountability, and
the desirability of institutional diversity complicate the matter of
public financing of private higher education.

The following section looks in detail at the patterns of financing
higher education in the New England states.

State and Local Support of Higher Education in New England

State and local appropriations for higher education in New England are allocated in a *pattern* similar to that in the United States
as a whole: Over 95 percent of these public funds go directly to
institutions (as opposed to individuals) in the form of student aid,
and over 97 percent of this institutional aid goes to the public
sector.

What distinguishes the financing of higher education in New
England from that of the country in general is the *level* of financing. In 1979 state and local per capita appropriations for
higher education in the region were 30 percent below the national
average ($61 per capita versus $87). This underfunding of higher
education by state and local governments in New England occurs
in both the private and public sectors. In the private sector in
1979, for instance, state and local appropriations in the region
amounted to $10 per FTE (full-time equivalent) student compared
with $100 nationally. Public sector institutions received $428 less
per student than the national average in state and local government
support that year, in spite of the lower proportion of students in
the region in the public sector. (See Table 3–2.) Rhode Island was
the only New England state that appropriated a greater than
average amount per student to its public institutions.

This low level of support of higher education in New England

Table 3–2   State and Local Appropriations* to Public Institutions of Higher Education in New England and the U.S., 1979 (per student)

State/Area	Universities	Professional and Specialized	Other 4-Year Colleges	2-Year Colleges	All Public Institutions
Conn.	$3,596	$55,239	$1,551	$1,342	$2,493
Maine	1,604	2,349	2,101	2,303	1,953
Mass.	3,914	4,098	2,069	1,323	2,269
N.H.	1,935	966	957	1,934	1,655
R.I.	3,233	—	2,744	2,137	2,803
Vt.	1,792	—	1,178	1,743	1,627
N.E.	2,974	4,771	1,921	1,453	2,266
U.S.	3,503	10,085	2,390	1,847	2,694

* Appropriations for current operating expenses only.

is *not* attributable to the particular mix of institutions in the region. In both the private and public sectors, for each institutional classification—universities, professional and specialized schools, other four-year colleges, and two-year colleges—regional appropriations per student fell short of the national averages.

The obvious explanation is inability to pay. This, however, does not appear to be the case for the region as a whole. While tax capacity (a measure of the potential of state and local governments to generate tax revenues) of four of the six New England states is below the national average and while Maine and New Hampshire, in particular, generate relatively low tax receipts, tax revenues per capita collected in the region have been considerably above average.[10] Three quarters of the region's students are in the two states that collect tax revenues per capita well in excess of the national average: Massachusetts, with tax revenues per capita 24 percent above the national average in 1979, and Connecticut, which was 12 percent above the national average. (See Table 3–3.)

Whatever weaknesses there may be in the region's economic base, a shortage of revenue *per se* does not appear to explain the low level of public resources available to higher education.[11] Instead, the explanation appears to be one of priorities. By almost any test, public resources going to higher education in New England are below that for the nation as a whole. As noted above, appropriations per capita by state and local governments were 30 percent below those for the United States in 1979. In addition, state and local government expenditures per capita on higher education in New England were 34 percent below the national

Table 3–3 State and Local Government Revenues and Allocations to Higher Education in New England, 1979

State/Area	State and Local Tax Capacity (per capita)	Tax Effort	State and Local Tax Revenues (per capita)	Percent Allocated Higher Education*	State and Local Appropriations to Higher Education* (per capita)
Conn.	$879	100%	$877	8%	$67
Maine	645	101	648	7	48
Mass.	727	133	966	6	61
N.H.	799	73	583	8	44
R.I.	684	114	779	9	72
Vt.	713	106	753	8	63
N.E.	759	114	866	7	61
U.S.	782	100	782	11	87

* Appropriations for current operating expenses only.

average.[12] (See Table 3–4.) Even taking into account the lesser role of public institutions relative to private institutions, New England still ranks low. On a per student basis in 1979, for example, state and local governments in New England appropriated 16 percent less to public institutions than did the nation as a whole. (See Table 3–2.)

By state, the same general patterns emerge, with some notable exceptions. State and local appropriations per capita to higher education in 1979 were below the national average in all six states. Expenditure data show one New England state, Vermont, spent above the national average per capita on higher education. On a per student basis, only Rhode Island appropriated more to its public institutions than the national average; all six states appropriated less per student in private institutions.

Institutional Financing in Higher Education

State and local appropriations are only one of several sources of revenue to institutions of higher education. The major alternative sources of support include tuition and fees, government grants and contracts, private gifts and grants, and endowments.

Institutional Revenues

Sharp distinctions exist between the region's public and private institutions in their reliance on these revenue sources. (See Table 3–5.) In the public sector, for instance, tuition and fees accounted for less than one fifth of institutional revenues in 1979, a distant second behind state and local appropriations (58 percent). Government grants and contracts to faculty in support of various research projects generated 15 percent of the public institutions' revenues, while private gifts, grants, and endowments jointly amounted to less than 3 percent of institutional support.

In contrast, private institutions are much more dependent on non-state sources of income. Although their total revenues were approximately double that of the public institutions in the region, private institutions received only one tenth of 1 percent of their institutional support from state and local appropriations. Tuition and fees generated one half of the private sector's revenues. Government grants and contracts to faculty accounted for over one

Table 3–4 State and Local Government Direct General Expenditures by Function for New England and the U.S., 1979 (per capita)

	Conn.	Maine	Mass.	N.H.	R.I.	Vt.	N.E.	U.S.
Higher education	$85 (6%)	$105 (8%)	$67 (4%)	$109 (9%)	$127 (8%)	$196 (13%)	$88 (6%)	$133 (9%)
Elementary and secondary education	$409 (29%)	$369 (28%)	$470 (28%)	$328 (27%)	$412 (26%)	$408 (27%)	$429 (28%)	$400 (27%)
Highways	$99 (7%)	$185 (14%)	$101 (6%)	$182 (15%)	$79 (5%)	$181 (12%)	$115 (8%)	$133 (9%)
Public welfare	$197 (14%)	$198 (15%)	$268 (16%)	$158 (13%)	$269 (17%)	$181 (12%)	$233 (15%)	$178 (12%)
Health and hospitals	$85 (6%)	$53 (4%)	$134 (8%)	$73 (6%)	$127 (8%)	$76 (5%)	$107 (7%)	$133 (9%)
Public service	$169 (12%)	$145 (11%)	$185 (11%)	$109 (9%)	$158 (10%)	$121 (8%)	$167 (11%)	$163 (11%)
Other	$381 (27%)	$277 (21%)	$453 (27%)	$255 (21%)	$396 (25%)	$332 (22%)	$396 (26%)	$326 (22%)
Total amount per capita	$1,425 (100%)	$1,318 (100%)	$1,678 (100%)	$1,214 (100%)	$1,568 (100%)	$1,495 (100%)	$1,534 (100%)	$1,466 (100%)

NOTE: Columns may not sum to 100% due to rounding.

Table 3–5 Distribution of Sources of Support* for Institutions of Higher Education in New England, by Sector, 1979

Source	Universities		Professional and Specialized		Other 4-year Colleges		2-Year Colleges		All	
	Public	Private	Public	Private	Public	Private	Public	Private	Public	Private
State and local appropriations	50%	†	73%	†	64%	†	68%	0%	58%	†
Tuition and fees	19	31	13	64	23	71	19	82	19	50
Private gifts, private grants and endowments	4	26	3	22	2	17	2	6	3	21
Government grants and contracts	20	34	6	7	10	7	8	7	15	22
Other	7	9	5	7	1	5	3	5	5	7
Total	100%	100%	100%	100%	100%	100%	100%	100%	100%	100%

* Educational and general institutional revenues only.
† Less than 1%.

fifth of private institutional support, while private gifts, grants, and endowments combined for another fifth.

Significant differences in the funding mix occur among types of institutions within each sector. For instance, state and local appropriations accounted for over two thirds of the public two-year colleges' revenues in the region in 1979 compared to only half of the public universities' income. The latter group of institutions generated much more income from government grants and contracts. In the private sector, New England universities had a diverse mix of support: 34 percent from government grants and contracts, 31 percent from tuition and fees, and 26 percent from private gifts, grants, and endowments. In contrast, private four-year and two-year colleges in the region were highly tuition-dependent, with 71 percent and 82 percent of their revenues, respectively, generated by tuition.

Tuition. In the private sector, regional tuition revenues per student for each classification of institution in 1979 exceeded the national average.[13] In the public sector, however, tuition revenues per student at professional and specialized institutions were below the national average. In addition, while on a regional basis tuition revenues per student at the public universities exceeded the national average, this was due to the extremely high tuition revenues of the public institutions in Vermont and New Hampshire. In Massachusetts and Connecticut, tuition revenues per student in public universities were well below average.

As implied above, there are vast differences in the importance of tuition revenues among the states in the region. Massachusetts, for example, has lower than average public sector tuition revenues per student (regionally and nationally) and higher than average private sector tuition revenues. Vermont and New Hampshire have unusually high tuition revenues per student throughout the public sector.

Students often seek financial assistance from the government to help meet the costs of higher education. In 1979 students and institutions in the New England states were allocated over $240 million dollars in federal student aid through the College Work-Study (CWS), Pell Grant (formerly the Basic Educational Opportunity Grant), and State Student Incentive Grant (SSIG) programs. In addition, almost $60 million in loans was committed by the federal government to students in New England in 1979 through the National Defense Student Loan (NDSL) and Guaranteed Student Loan (GSL) programs.[14]

Government Grants and Contracts. Government grants and contracts, the majority of which come from federal funds in support of research and development, are an important source of institutional support of higher education in New England. In fact, in 1979, higher education in New England (public and private combined) received almost as much financial support from government grants and contracts as it did from state and local appropriations.

Throughout the 1970s New England colleges and universities received a relatively stable and disproportionately large share of all federal R&D grants.[15] Massachusetts, in particular, consistently ranked third highest in R&D allocations in the country, after California and New York. Universities in both the public and private sectors receive significant proportions of their revenues from government grants and contracts. However, almost three quarters of the government grants and contracts awarded to faculty in New England in 1979 went to the private sector.

Private Gifts, Grants, and Endowments. Private gifts, grants, and endowments provided 15 percent of the institutional support of higher education in New England in 1979. The private sector received the bulk (94 percent) of these funds.

Disaggregated data on the composition of private gifts and grants are not available on a regional basis. However, nationally, individual contributions comprise about half of the voluntary support of higher education. Foundations are the next largest source, followed by corporations.[16] This pattern has been relatively stable in the past decade. Foundations and corporations tend to concentrate their support on the major private universities and the large public institutions. Individual support is more broadly dispersed although, at least in the private sector, a few large donations account for the bulk of individual contributions. In academic year 1973–1974, for instance, less than 1 percent of the gifts comprised 72 percent of the total amount contributed by individuals to private institutions of higher education.[17]

Voluntary support to private institutions far outweighs that to public institutions. However, in recent years such support to public institutions has been growing more rapidly.[18]

Institutional Expenditure Patterns

Institutions of higher education in New England spend a lower proportion of their revenues on instruction and on public service than is true nationally, while a slightly higher share of their bud-

Table 3–6 Expenditures* of Institutions of Higher Education in New England Relative to the U.S. Average, by Sector, 1979

Expenditures	Universities		Professional and Specialized		Other 4-Year Colleges		2-Year Colleges		All	
	Public	Private	Public	Private	Public	Private	Public	Private	Public	Private
Instruction (per student)	−17%	−11%	−59%	−31%	−25%	+ 6%	−25%	+ 10%	−21%	+ 4%
Academic support (per student)	+ 5%	+20%	−58%	−36%	− 8%	+ 9%	−19%	− 23%	− 8%	+29%
Research (per faculty member)	−40%	+20%	−96%	+ 1%	−68%	+16%	−93%	−100%	−34%	+53%
Public service (per 1,000 capita)	−42%	+ 2%	−22%	+59%	−70%	+27%	−58%	+ 7%	−46%	+31%
Other E&G (per student)	+17%	+19%	−32%	−16%	−18%	+ 8%	−18%	+ 17%	− 1%	+18%
Total E&G expenditures (per student)	− 9%	+ 7%	−52%	−34%	−23%	+ 7%	−22%	+ 9%	−14%	+18%

* Educational and general (E&G) expenditures.

gets goes to academic support services.[19] Private, but not public, institutions in the region allocate a larger percentage of their budgets to research than the national average.

Dollar amounts of such spending are more revealing. For instance, low revenues received by the region's public institutions resulted in total expenditures per student $615 below the national average in 1979. (See Appendix, Table 3A–4.) Relatively low total expenditure levels occurred across institutional categories in the public sector. Moreover, average expenditure levels in the public sector fell below national averages in each spending category— instruction, academic support, research, public service, and other educational and general (E&G) expenditures. (See Table 3–6.) In contrast, the region's private institutions on average spent $1,058 more per student on total expenditures than the national average. Only at the professional and specialized level were total expenditures per student lower in the region than in the nation. In marked contrast to the region's public sector, private colleges and universities overall spent above the national average in all aspects of educational services, from instruction to public service.

The following sections review the relative magnitudes of these regional expenditure differences and highlight state and institutional variation in New England in 1979.

Instructional Expenditures. Instructional expenditures accounted for over 40 percent of the budget in the region's public institutions and one third of the private sector's budget. The region's public institutions spent 21 percent ($398) less per student on instruction than the national average. Less money was spent on instruction across institutional classification in the public sector.

The regional average of instructional expenditures per student in the private sector was 4 percent ($88) above the national norm. However, while the private four-year and two-year colleges spent above-average amounts on student instruction, the region's private universities and professional and specialized institutions had below-average instructional expenditures per student. Even so, New England's private universities on average spent over 60 percent ($1,306) more per student on instruction than did the area's public universities. Private four-year colleges in the region spent 38 percent ($497) more on student instruction than the public four-year colleges. At the professional and specialized level, public institutions spent about twice as much on instruction per student as did private institutions.

Of the New England states, only Vermont's public institutions spent more on student instruction than the national average. (See Appendix, Table 3A–5.) Massachusetts had the lowest level of instructional expenditures in the region in the public sector, followed by Maine. Connecticut had unusually high instructional expenditures per student ($31,105) in its public professional and specialized institutions. Connecticut also had relatively high student instructional expenditures ($8,670) in its private universities—an amount over four times greater than that for the state's public universities.

Academic Support. Ten percent of the higher education budgets in the region's public institutions went to academic support services.[20] The comparable figure for the private sector was 9 percent. The region's public institutions spent 8 percent ($45) less per student on academic support than the national norm. Academic support per student in the region's private sector was 29 percent ($139) above the national average. The region's private professional and specialized institutions and two-year colleges, however, spent considerably less than the national average on academic support.

In the public sector, academic support was particularly high in Rhode Island, bolstered by such spending in the four-year colleges. (See Appendix, Table 3A–6.) Private institutions overall in New Hampshire, Connecticut, and Massachusetts spent well above the U.S. average on academic support.

Public Service. Public service expenditures accounted for 4 percent of the budget in New England's public sector institutions, compared with only 1 percent of the private sector spending. In 1979 the region's public institutions overall spent 46 percent ($2,806 per thousand capita) below the national average for public institutions. However, while they accounted for a minority of the region's institutions and enrollments in higher education, public institutions spent more than twice the amount on public service than was spent by private institutions. This was true in spite of the fact that New England's private institutions spent over 30 percent more per capita than did the same group nationwide. In both the public and private sectors, the universities accounted for over two thirds of the public service expenditures.

Institutional public service expenditures per capita vary widely among the New England states. (See Appendix, Table 3A–7.) In Vermont, for instance, public institutions spent $12,998 per thou-

sand capita—more than double the public sector national average
and almost four-fold the regional average for public institutions.
Public institutions in Maine also spent above the national norm
on public service.

Massachusetts alone was responsible for the higher than average
regional statistics on public service spending by private institutions. This state's private colleges and universities spent $2,658
per thousand capita on public service in 1979—an amount more
than double the national average.

Research.   Ten percent of the spending of public institutions
of higher education in New England was devoted to research, as
was 17 percent of the private sector's budget. Research expenditures by institutions of higher education in New England are
highly correlated with the revenues received from government
grants and contracts. As noted earlier, New England's institutions
of higher education, particularly its universities, receive a disproportionately large share of federal funds for research—the bulk
(75 percent) of which goes to the private sector. The result in
1979 was research expenditures of $7,895 per faculty member in
the public sector in New England, $4,127 less than the U.S.
average; and $24,959 per faculty member in the private sector in
the region, $8,675 more than the U.S. average.

The universities were responsible for over 80 percent of the
region's research expenditures in higher education. Private universities in Massachusetts alone accounted for over half of the
research spending in the region—the equivalent of $57,072 per
faculty member in Massachusetts' private universities. Private
universities in Connecticut spent $58,521 per faculty member on
research. (See Appendix, Table 3A–8.)

In the remaining four New England states, public institutions
spent more per faculty member on research than did private
institutions. In Vermont, for instance, public institutions spent
$15,484 per faculty member, approximately 30 percent above the
national average for public institutions; the comparable figure in
Vermont's private institutions was $526.

Other "E&G" Expenditures.   Institutional support (general administration services and planning), student services, operation
and maintenance of plant, educational and general mandatory
transfers and scholarships and fellowships awarded by institutions
are included in the "other E&G expenditures" category.

Public institutions of higher education in New England, in each institutional classification except the universities, spent less per student for such expenditures than the national average. For the region's private institutions, such expenditures were 18 percent above the national norm, with only the professional and specialized institutional category below the U.S. average.

Other "E&G" expenditures were recorded by the National Institute of Education and the National Center for Higher Education Management Systems in the aggregate, thus prohibiting detailed analysis of these components in this chapter.

Policy Implications

The financing of higher education in the 1980s is a critical issue for both public and private colleges and universities. The decade ahead promises to be a particularly challenging one: In contrast to the growth environment of the 1960s and early 1970s, most institutions of higher education will be operating in a milieu threatened by declining enrollments and vast reductions of federal support.

A critical point developed in this chapter is that New England, relative to the national averages, maintains a conspicuous pattern of underfunding by state and local governments of both public and private higher education. This is particularly harmful to the public institutions in the region as they are highly dependent on state and local appropriations for revenues. The private institutions in New England have never received much financial support from state and local tax revenues. However, institutional revenues at private institutions are highly susceptible to enrollment declines, which threaten tuition income, cuts in federal student aid, and declines in government R&D support.

Two categories of policies that address the financial concerns of institutions of higher education in New England will be discussed next: first, increased funding to higher education, and second, more efficient use of the funds available to higher education.

Increased Funding Through State and Local Appropriations

In the past, state and local tax revenues per capita in New England have been above the national average. In the region, only New

Hampshire has a tax effort that is below the U.S. average. Public discontent with high taxes has risen steadily, as seen most clearly in the passage of Proposition 2½ in Massachusetts. These developments suggest that raising tax rates to generate additional monies for higher education is likely to meet resistance. Alternatively, additional tax revenues could be generated by expanding the region's relatively weak economic tax base—that is, increasing the states' taxable capacity by attracting more industry through economic development programs. The revenue-generating effects of such programs, however, are not felt immediately and depend very much on the overall health of the economy.

A more immediate solution is for the states to reorder their budget and spending priorities. All six of the New England states allocate a smaller proportion of their state and local tax revenues to higher education than the national average. In 1979 state and local government expenditures per capita on higher education were below average in five of the six states, resulting in a regional expenditure level one third below the national average.

For years higher education in New England has taken a back seat to other public expenditures. This may be explained in part by the presence of the strong private sector in higher education in the region, particularly in Massachusetts. The fact remains, however, that almost a quarter of a million of the region's residents attend public institutions of higher education in New England. Yet these institutions are receiving state and local governmental funding per student well below the national average and are spending less per student than the U.S. norm on all aspects of educational services, from instruction to public service. Clearly this is an area ripe for building public awareness.

Other Sources of Support of Higher Education

An alternative way to increase funding to higher education in the region is to expand other sources of support to colleges and universities.

Tuition. Tuition revenues per student in the private sector in New England are already high relative to the country as a whole. In addition, tuition revenues per student in the public sector in Vermont, New Hampshire, Maine, and Rhode Island are above the national norms. Tuition revenues per student in Massachusetts and Connecticut, however, are for the most part well below average. For instance, in Massachusetts in 1979, tuition revenues per student in public universities were 75 percent below the U.S. average; in professional and specialized institutions, 61 percent below; and in four-year colleges, 21 percent below. In Connecticut, while public four-year colleges had tuition revenues per student 12 percent above the national average, tuition revenues per student in the public universities were 42 percent below average and were 16 percent below average in the public two-year colleges.

One obvious reason for relatively low tuition revenues per student may be low tuition *levels*. Alternatively, tuition revenues may be low because tuition is simply not collected from some students—for instance, as a result of a tuition waiver program for the needy. Data for the academic year 1979–1980 indicate that public sector tuition levels in Connecticut and Massachusetts are low relative to those found in Vermont and New Hampshire. However, by national standards these tuition levels often exceed the norm. (See Appendix Table 3A–9.)

Where tuition levels are below the national average, tuition increases are an obvious revenue source. Given overall under-funding of public higher education in the region, such bargain tuitions are hard to justify. States that have low tuition revenues because they provide an unusually large number of tuition waivers, however, can increase their tuition income only by raising tuition further or by tightening eligibility for tuition waivers.

It should be noted, however, that in some states, higher tuition levels may not yield higher income for the institutions involved even if enrollments are maintained. For instance, in Massachusetts, tuition income is treated as part of the state's general revenues. In states where there is no direct link between tuitions and the higher education budget, tuition increases alone cannot ensure expanded resources to higher education.

Grants and Contracts. Public institutions in the region have been far less successful in attracting sponsored research than their private sector counterparts. However, recently, there have been significant cutbacks in the total number of federal dollars allocated to R&D and this trend is expected to continue. These funds cannot, therefore, be a reliable source of "bailouts" of higher education.

Private Gifts, Grants, and Endowments. Future support of higher education from private gifts, grants, and endowments does not look optimistic either. Endowments in public institutions are minimal. In recent years private institutions have watched the value of their endowment incomes shrink in the face of relatively high rates of inflation. Private gifts and grants were slightly higher in real terms per student and as a percentage of institutional expenditures in 1978–1979 than in 1974–1975.[21] However, the 1978–1979 level was significantly below that of the 1960s and the early 1970s. Individual contributions, which comprise about half of the voluntary support to higher education, are expected to fall in response to recent changes in the tax law that make these donations "more expensive" for high-income individuals, who are responsible for the bulk of individual support.[22]

Corporate contributions to institutions of higher education in the United States have been rising in recent years; however, such support accounts for less than 3 percent of total support of higher education.[23] Substantial increases in corporate giving would be necessary to make even a small improvement in higher education financing.

Efficient Resource Allocation

The second category of educational policy implications involves policies geared to a more efficient use of the resources available to higher education. To have a strong and viable system of higher education in the 1990s we should encourage and reward excellence and high-quality programs—both within states and among states. In the face of contracting enrollments and limited resources in higher education, it is generally recognized that the time has come for systemwide reorganization. Interschool consortia, elimination of duplicate programs, school closings, mergers, systemwide exchanges of faculty and students, and shared equipment and facilities have all been discussed as options for such reorganization.[24]

The significant degree of diversity in higher education among the New England states indicates that no one policy or package of policies will be appropriate to deal with the various problems and issues facing higher education in the region. Therefore, each state must develop and coordinate its own reorganization scheme around the students and institutions in that particular state. Where commonalities exist among the states and when quality can be improved or wasteful duplication eliminated with interstate resource allocation, regional planning and coordination should be utilized.

Obviously, all of the options available for reorganizing higher education in New England cannot be dealt with here. However, a couple of policies that directly link reorganization with issues of tuition and financing are worth commenting on briefly.

A Public Sector Voucher System. A variety of economic and political factors determine resource allocation and the resulting mix of programs and institutions in higher education. Nevertheless, there is widespread agreement that student preferences should and do play a key role in this process. In the private sector, for example, student choice among competing schools clearly influences institutional survival. In the public sector, however, public funding priorities can weaken the influence of student choice.

It is frequently proposed that students be given wider influence over educational priorities through voucher systems which would grant scholarship students complete freedom of choice in allocating their tuition payments among all institutions. A less common, and perhaps original suggestion, is that of the establishment of a public sector voucher system. Under such a system the states could establish a new student aid program organized around vouchers to students—vouchers to be used only at the public institutions of their choice.

Restricting vouchers to the public sector, at least initially, would provide time for reorganization of the public sector. The goal would be a financially more viable public system with student demands propelling any changes. Subsequently, vouchers might be used in the private sector as well, to promote further reorganization through expanded competition between the two sectors.

Portability of State Aid. In the past, New England has been a leader in allowing state scholarships and grants to be "portable." That is, as long as students maintain their residence in their home state, they may take their student aid awards to the institution and state of their choice. In the past few years, however, there has been a trend toward "reciprocity." Reciprocity is a restricted form of portability whereby residents of one state may take their student aid only to those states that allow their students reciprocal privileges.

Currently in New England, only Vermont and Rhode Island have "portable" student aid. Massachusetts and Connecticut recently switched from portable to reciprocal arrangements. In response, Maine and New Hampshire, states that in the past had neither portable nor reciprocal arrangements, have passed laws allowing for reciprocal student aid contracts.

Left to their own devices, states can be expected to develop parochial policies with respect to student aid in higher education. New England as a region has a strong interest in programs that encourage and reward interstate mobility and portability of student aid. The region would benefit from the more efficient allocation of resources with elimination or prevention of unnecessary program duplication. In addition, given the importance of out-of-state students, institutions of higher education in the region stand to gain on the revenue side as well.

Programs such as the Regional Student Program sponsored by the New England Board of Higher Education (NEBHE), in which New England residents may attend public institutions in other New England states at the resident tuition level or at a reduced rate, are a step toward reversing the decline in student mobility. NEBHE also runs a Regional Contract Program encouraging interstate utilization of a limited number of health training programs in the region. More needs to be done, however, in involving a greater number of states and the private sector in promoting student mobility and flexibility within the higher education system.

Epilogue

We are currently witnessing a reversal of the fifty-year trend of an expanding role of the federal government in higher education. In New England, the decline in federal funds to higher education will place greater financial strain on a system already hampered by underfunding by state and local governments. This strain will require changes in both the financing and reorganization of higher education in the region. The states' role in planning and financing higher education will be critical.

While states may choose to increase their allocation of revenues to higher education, it seems inevitable in the search for additional monies in some states that tuition levels in the public sector will need to be increased. Higher tuitions, however, undermine accessibility of higher education to students in low income families.

Student aid, bolstered in the past by the federal government, is important for both access and freedom of choice in higher education. While federal funds for student assistance have risen significantly in the past decade, such funds are slated for vast reduction under the Reagan Administration.[25] If tuitions are raised to generate additional revenues but are not accompanied by need-based student aid programs, the opportunity to pursue higher education will be seriously threatened. Also, if student choice is to play a key role in reorganization, students must have available the resources to enable them to attend the institution of their choice.

Will the New England states buck tradition and reallocate a larger share of their budgets to higher education? Can the trend away from portability of student aid be reversed? Are the states willing to counter tradition and significantly alter the composition of their support—increasing student aid possibly at the expense of institutional aid? Will the states be flexible not only in reshaping the financing of the public sector, but also in integrating the private sector in overall reorganization?

The future of higher education in New England depends on the capabilities of the states to meet these challenges.

Endnotes

1. This chapter is concerned exclusively with the financing of *operating* budgets of higher education. The financing of physical plant and equipment assets are subject to a different set of funding arrangements and decision-making criteria. In this paper, data on state and local appropriations are for current operating expenses only; thus total appropriation figures are understated by the amount of capital support. Institutional revenues in this chapter are for education and general ("E&G") revenues only.

   Unless otherwise noted, this paper is based on unpublished data from the National Center for Higher Education Management Systems (NCHEMS) and the National Institute of Education (NIE). Their data source was primarily the Higher Education General Information Survey (HEGIS) for 1979. These data will soon be published for each of the states in Marilyn McCoy and D. Kent Halstead, *Financing Higher Education in the Fifty States, FY 1979* (Washington, D.C.: National Institute of Education), forthcoming.

   It has been brought to the author's attention that the HEGIS data for Massachusetts includes some continuing education students in the enrollment data but not in the institutional revenues. The net result is an understatement of per student figures, although the exact amount is not known.

2. For a review of trends in higher education in New England since World War II, see Peter B. Doeringer, Patricia Flynn Pannell, and Pankaj Tandon, "Market Influences on Higher Education: A Perspective for the 1980s," in

John C. Hoy and Melvin H. Bernstein (eds.), *Business and Academia: Partners in New England's Economic Renewal* (Hanover, N.H.: University Press of New England, 1981), pp. 26–74.

3. This chapter combines major categories in the NCHEMS institutional classification system as follows: Universities—includes major doctoral degree universities without medical programs and those with medical programs that are integrated within a campus at the university. For this study, institutions classified as research universities and as universities were combined. Professional and Specialized—includes (1) health professional institutions that grant degrees in a variety of medical first-professional areas and (2) a mixed group of other professional and specialized institutions, including single program medical schools, engineering schools, teachers colleges, law schools, and seminaries. Other Four-Year Colleges—includes (1) comprehensive institutions in which graduate degrees are primarily master's level and (2) baccalaureate institutions where most degrees are at the bachelor's level. Two-Year Colleges—institutions which confer associate or certificate degrees but not bachelor's, master's or doctoral level degrees.

4. National Center for Educational Statistics, *Residence and Migration of College Students* (Washington, D.C.: U.S. Government Printing Office, Fall 1979), Table 1.

In contrast to past years, as of fall 1979 student migration data published by the National Center for Education Statistics (NCES) refer only to new students. Thus, "migrating student" refers to a student who enrolls for the first time at an institution in a state other than his/her home state.

5. Carnegie Foundation for the Advancement of Teaching, *More Than Survival* (San Francisco, Cal.: Jossey-Bass Publishers, 1975), pp. 1–3; John C. Honey and Donna Clark, *Federal Leadership for a More Effective Partnership in Post-Secondary Education* (New York: Syracuse Research Corporation, May 1977), pp. 1–29.

6. Alice Rivlin, *The Role of the Federal Government in Financing Higher Education*, (Washington, D.C.: The Brookings Institution, 1961), pp. 68–69; Joseph Golden, *The Best Years, 1945–1950* (New York: Atheneum, 1976), pp. 66–68.

7. Honey and Clark, *op. cit.*, pp. 18–19; *The Second Newman Report: National Policy and Higher Education* (Cambridge, Mass.: MIT Press, 1975); Carnegie Commission on Higher Education, *Higher Education: Who Pays? Who Should Pay?* (New York: McGraw Hill, 1973).

8. Honey and Clark, *op. cit.*, pp. 21–22.

9. A. E. Dick Howard, *State Aid to Private Higher Education* (Charlottesville, Va.: The Michie Company, 1977), pp. 1–15.

In Supreme Court decisions a major distinction has been made between primary and secondary level education and higher education. For instance, public aid to church-related colleges or universities is less likely to be found unconstitutional than such aid to primary or secondary levels. This is because it is believed that college students are "less impressionable and less susceptible to religious indoctrination" than are younger students and that college courses would limit sectarian influences and are characterized by a high degree of academic freedom.

10. "Tax capacity" refers to the potential state and local tax revenues. It represents the amount that state and local governments could raise, relative to other state and local governments, if they all applied rates at the national average to their tax bases. "Tax effort" refers to the extent to which a state makes use of its fiscal taxable capacity. See Marilyn McCoy and D. Kent Halstead, *Higher Education Financing in the Fifty States, FY 1976* (Washington, D.C.: U.S. Government Printing Office, Fall 1979), Table 1.

11. New England differed from the United States in its reliance on the property tax. For instance, in 1977, the property tax generated almost half (49%) of the state and local tax revenues in New England compared to 36% nationally. There was also a greater regional dependence on the corporate income tax. In contrast, the individual income tax and the general sales tax accounted for less than proportional shares of regional tax revenues. (See Appendix, Tables 3A–2 and 3A–3.)

12. Direct general expenditures include federal revenue sharing monies and any other funds states receive beyond state and local tax revenues.

13. Tuition and fees are available by institution but are not readily available on a statewide basis by sector and institutional classification. Tuition revenues per student, reported by HEGIS, represent all institutional revenues collected from tuition and fees, including amounts remitted to the state as an offset to the state appropriations, divided by the institution's full time equivalent enrollment.

14. Office of Student Financial Assistance, U.S. Department of Education, *OSFA Program Book* (Washington, D.C.: U.S. Government Printing Office, July 1981), pp. 5–8.

15. See Doeringer et al., *op. cit.*, pp. 26–74.

16. Council for Financial Aid to Education, *Voluntary Support of Education, 1978–79* (New York: Council for Financial Aid to Education, 1980), pp. 3–10.

17. Susan C. Nelson, "Financial Trends and Issues," in David W. Breneman and Chester E. Finn, Jr. (eds.), *Public Policy and Private Higher Education* (Washington, D.C.: The Brookings Institution, 1978), p. 69.

18. Council of Financial Aid to Education, *op. cit.*, p. 10.

19. Academic support includes expenditures for the support services that are an integral part of the institution's primary missions of instruction, research, or public service. It includes expenditures for libraries, museums, galleries, audiovisual services, academic computing support, ancillary support, academic administration, personnel development, and course and curriculum development.

20. Public service includes all funds budgeted specifically for public service and expended for activities established primarily to provide noninstructional services beneficial to groups external to the institution. It includes expenditures for seminars and projects provided to particular sectors of the community, community services, and cooperative extension services.

21. Council for Financial Aid to Education, *op. cit.*, p. 6.

22. The Economic Recovery Tax Act of 1981 lowers the marginal tax rates in the upper income brackets and is expected to cause charitable contributions to fall since the cost of giving is now higher. The tax treatment of charitable

contributions has improved for lower income individuals who did not itemize. However, it is unlikely that additional contributions from these low income individuals would outweigh the loss from declines in upper income individual contributions. Also, if past trends continue, charitable contributions of low income individuals are more likely to go to the church than to higher education.

See Emil M. Sunley, Jr., "Federal and State Tax Policies," in Breneman and Finn, *op. cit.*, pp. 281–319, for a review of studies on tax incentives and giving.

23. Council for Financial Aid to Education, *op. cit.*, p. 59.
24. See for instance, David W. Breneman and Chester E. Finn, Jr., "An Agenda for the Eighties," in Breneman and Finn, *op. cit.*, pp. 411–450. also in that volume see Colin C. Blaydon, "State Policy Options," pp. 353–388; Robert W. Hartman, "Federal Options for Student Aid," pp. 231–279; and Robert O. Berdahl, "The Policies of State Aid," pp. 321–352. Peter B. Doeringer et al., *op. cit.*; Kenneth P. Mortimer and Michael L. Tierney, *The Three "R's" of the Eighties: Reduction, Reallocation and Retrenchment* (Washington, D.C.: American Association for Higher Education, 1979); Carnegie Council on Policy Studies in Higher Education, *The States and Private Higher Education* (San Francisco, Cal.: Jossey-Bass Publishers, 1977).
25. Agencies such as the Rhode Island Higher Education Assistance Authority, the Vermont Assistance Corporation, and the Massachusetts Higher Education Assistance Corporation have been established to assist students in financing higher education. These agencies vary by state, but are generally responsible for informing the public about sources of financial aid and for administering various state scholarship, grant, and loan programs.

Federal cutbacks in student aid further threaten state-provided student aid. Some states, for instance, will cut back or eliminate their State Student Incentive Program (SSIG) if the matching federal dollars are not forthcoming. The bulk of state assistance that goes directly to students will most likely continue to be in the form of student loans.

APPENDIX: SUPPLEMENTARY DATA

Table 3A–1   Institutions of Higher Education in New England, by State, 1979

	Conn.	Maine	Mass.	N.H.	R.I.	Vt.	N.E.
Public							
Universities	1	1	1	1	1	1	6
Professional and specialized	1	4	4	1	0	0	10
Other 4-year colleges	4	3	10	1	1	3	22
2-year colleges	<u>16</u>	<u>2</u>	<u>18</u>	<u>7</u>	<u>1</u>	<u>2</u>	<u>46</u>
All public institutions	22	10	33	10	3	6	84
Private							
Universities	1	0	8	1	1	0	11
Professional and specialized	7	6	25	3	3	4	48
Other 4-year colleges	12	8	28	6	5	9	68
2-year colleges	<u>5</u>	<u>3</u>	<u>25</u>	<u>4</u>	<u>1</u>	<u>2</u>	<u>40</u>
All private institutions	25	17	86	14	10	15	167
Total, public and private institutions	47	27	119	24	13	21	251

Table 3A–2 Tax Revenues Collected by the New England States and the U.S., 1977 (per capita)

	Conn.	Maine	Mass.	N.H.	R.I.	Vt.	U.S.
Individual Taxes							
Individual income tax	$ 19	$ 69	$206	$ 8	$111	$146	$135
Residential property tax	244	145	284	235	193	196	104
Corporate Taxes							
Corporate net income tax	65	32	69	38	44	35	43
Commercial and industrial property taxes	133	67	163	110	109	84	103
Other Taxes							
General sales taxes	188	156	76	0	152	67	168
Selective sales taxes and gross receipts	151	116	99	115	121	125	103
Farm and public utility property taxes	36	26	44	38	19	51	40
Death, gift, severance, and license taxes	42	36	25	40	32	49	48
All taxes	$878	$647	$966	$584	$781	$753	$744

Table 3A–3 Distribution of State and Local Government Tax Sources in New England and the U.S., 1977

Tax	Conn.	Maine	Mass.	N.H.	R.I.	Vt.	N.E.	U.S.
Property tax	47%	37%	51%	66%	41%	44%	49%	36%
Individual income tax	2	11	21	1	14	19	14	17
Corporate income tax	7	5	7	7	6	5	7	6
General sales tax	21	24	8	0	20	9	13	22
Selective sales and gross receipts	17	18	10	20	16	17	14	13
Other*	5	6	3	7	4	7	4	6
Total	100%	100%	100%	100%	100%	100%	100%	100%

NOTE: Columns may not sum to 100% due to rounding.
* Death, gift, severance, and license taxes.

Table 3A–4 Total Expenditures in Higher Education in the New England States, by Institutional Classification, 1979 (per student)

State/Area	Universities	Professional and Specialized	Other 4-Year Colleges	2-Year Colleges	All Institutions
Conn.	$ 5,626	$77,140	$2,410	$1,765	$3,700
	($21,857)*	($5,786)	($4,539)	($1,800)	($8,315)
Maine	5,379	3,721	6,994	3,559	4,474
	—	(3,794)	(6,207)	(1,903)	(5,228)
Mass.	5,437	5,267	2,594	1,824	3,001
	(10,198)	(4,273)	(4,835)	(3,039)	(7,424)
N.H.	5,931	3,169	3,026	2,531	4,525
	(15,959)	(2,175)	(3,492)	(4,031)	(6,431)
R.I.	6,528	—	3,876	2,811	4,825
	(9,040)	(2,854)	(3,472)	(2,105)	(4,698)
Vt.	7,521	—	3,172	2,767	5,933
	—	(4,449)	(4,949)	(2,935)	(4,709)
N.E.	5,921	6,917	2,758	1,974	3,722
	(11,333)	(3,765)	(4,655)	(2,892)	(7,081)
U.S.	6,500	14,334	3,603	2,534	4,337
	(10,557)	(5,664)	(4,334)	(2,732)	(6,023)

* Figures for private institutions are in parentheses.

Table 3A–5 Instructional Expenditures in Higher Education in the New England States and the U.S., by Institutional Classification, 1979 (per student)

State/Area	Universities	Professional and Specialized	Other 4-Year Colleges	2-Year Colleges	All Institutions
Conn.	$2,065	$31,105	$1,240	$ 737	$1,538
	($8,670)*	($1,854)	($1,931)	($1,117)	($3,369)
Maine	1,481	1,509	1,421	2,214	1,518
	—	(1,205)	(1,893)	(397)	(1,592)
Mass.	2,165	2,068	1,249	888	1,340
	(2,799)	(1,655)	(1,847)	(1,020)	(2,254)
N.H.	1,663	1,291	1,290	1,566	1,539
	(5,087)	(773)	(1,270)	(1,419)	(2,145)
R.I.	2,123	—	1,662	1,407	1,807
	(3,386)	(1,116)	(1,243)	(988)	(1,758)
Vt.	3,151	—	1,426	1,395	2,534
	—	(1,394)	(1,815)	(887)	(1,681)
N.E.	2,111	2,768	1,293	953	1,521
	(3,417)	(1,415)	(1,790)	(1,014)	(2,331)
U.S.	2,548	6,704	1,730	1,272	1,919
	(3,837)	(2,046)	(1,689)	(926)	(2,243)

* Figures for private institutions are in parentheses.

Table 3A–6   Academic Support Expenditures in Higher Education in the New England States and the U.S., by Institutional Classification, 1979 (per student)

State/Area	Universities	Professional and Specialized	Other 4-Year Colleges	2-Year Colleges	All Institutions
Conn.	$ 706	$5,813	$207	$182	$385
	($1,946)*	($541)	($342)	($207)	($693)
Maine	357	275	426	49	313
	—	(326)	(521)	(238)	(447)
Mass.	506	336	320	153	298
	(906)	(284)	(440)	(125)	(639)
N.H.	513	384	284	242	414
	(2,262)	(240)	(322)	(233)	(801)
R.I.	692	—	787	162	566
	(754)	(187)	(149)	(6)	(321)
Vt.	598	—	218	299	470
	—	(677)	(397)	(224)	(417)
N.E.	634	517	315	167	362
	(1,036)	(281)	(384)	(145)	(613)
U.S.	604	1,218	343	207	393
	(864)	(436)	(332)	(189)	(474)

* Figures for private institutions are in parentheses.

Table 3A–7   Public Service Expenditures in the New England States, by Institutional Classification, 1979 (per 1,000 capita)

State/Area	Universities	Professional and Specialized	Other 4-Year Colleges	2-Year Colleges	All Institutions
Conn.	$1,830	$170	$ 0	$721	$2,721
	($0)*	($71)	($642)	($5)	($718)
Maine	5,724	962	1,200	0	7,886
	—	(0)	(48)	(0)	(48)
Mass.	1,276	432	122	61	1,891
	(2,133)	(178)	(325)	(22)	(2,658)
N.H.	3,269	2	0	19	3,290
	(699)	(0)	(280)	(1)	(980)
R.I.	3,974	—	415	0	4,389
	(0)	(746)	(0)	(0)	(746)
Vt.	12,283	—	654	61	12,998
	—	(56)	(0)	(75)	(131)
N.E.	2,590	332	222	216	3,360
	(1,056)	(161)	(340)	(15)	(1,572)
U.S.	4,465	428	756	517	6,166
	(524)	(391)	(268)	(14)	(1,197)

* Figures for private institutions are in parentheses.

Table 3A–8   Research Expenditures in the New England States, by Institutional Classification, 1979 (per faculty member)

State/Area	Universities	Professional and Specialized	Other 4-Year Colleges	2-Year Colleges	All Institutions
Conn.	$12,582	$0	$0	$0	$ 7,909
	($58,521)*	($1,759)	($3,861)	($0)	($21,088)
Maine	21,704	197	5,224	0	10,603
	—	(0)	(1,207)	(0)	(955)
Mass.	11,838	1,321	614	16	3,668
	(57,072)	(5,679)	(1,882)	(0)	(31,975)
N.H.	30,293	9,694	7,507	0	18,267
	(30,186)	(1,613)	(46)	(0)	(13,407)
R.I.	25,723	—	0	0	12,209
	(25,546)	(0)	(137)	(0)	(11,988)
Vt.	24,019	—	0	0	15,484
	—	(1,206)	(413)	(0)	(526)
N.E.	18,165	2,831	898	8	7,895
	(53,566)	(3,781)	(2,085)	(0)	(24,959)
U.S.	30,116	64,013	2,811	299	12,022
	(44,462)	(3,757)	(1,797)	(120)	(16,284)

* Figures for private institutions are in parentheses.

Table 3A–9 Undergraduate Tuition and Required Fees at Selected Public Institutions in New England and the U.S., 1979–1980

	1979–1980 Tuition and Fees In State/Out-of-State ($)	Highest Degree Granted
Connecticut		
University of Connecticut	1020/1710	doctorate
Central Conn. State College	726/1716	master's
Western Conn. State College	724/1714	master's
Regional Community Colleges	354/1054	associate
Maine		
University of Maine/Orono	920/2713	doctorate
University of Maine/Presque Isle	820/2642	bachelor's
Massachusetts		
Univ. of Mass./Amherst	992/2552	doctorate
Univ. of Mass./Boston	674/2200	master's
Univ. of Lowell	735/2315	doctorate
Bridgewater State College	698/2198	master's
Massasoit Community College	453/1514	associate
Roxbury Community College	488/1547	associate
New Hampshire		
Univ. of New Hampshire	1150/3700	doctorate
Keene State College	973/2673	master's
Plymouth State College	978/2678	master's
Rhode Island		
Univ. of Rhode Island	1097/2733	doctorate
Rhode Island College	730/2033	master's
Community College of R.I.	464/—	associate
Vermont		
Univ. of Vermont	1662/4312	doctorate
Castleton State College	1100/2680	master's
Lyndon State College	1100/2680	master's
Community College of Vt.	500/1000	associate
United States—Averages		
Public Universities	810/2166	
Public 4-year colleges	660/1692	
Public 2-year colleges	405/1153	

SOURCES: State Tuition and Fee Schedules, Bursar's Office, Department of Higher Education.

U.S. Averages: Resident and Nonresident Undergraduate and Graduate Tuition and Required Fees, Jan. 1982 Council for Postsecondary Education.

Chapter 4

THE SYSTEM OF HIGHER EDUCATION IN NEW ENGLAND

by Jean Mayer and Robert W. Eisenmenger

The papers of Professors Patricia F. Pannell and Michael S. McPherson presented at NEBHE's January 1982 Conference on Tax Policy and Higher Education elicited much comment from participants. The most extensive responses came from Dr. Jean Mayer, President of Tufts University, and from Robert W. Eisenmenger, Senior Vice President and Director of Research at the Federal Reserve Bank of Boston. Each emphasized the unique problems and strengths New England higher education gains from its combination of public and private institutions. Both educator and economist stressed the need for a regional plan to concentrate scarce resources, first by seeing all New England colleges and universities as a single system, and second by creating "centers of excellence" in each academic field while eliminating wasteful, overlapping programs.

Jean Mayer: Tailoring Educational Programs to Meet Regional Needs

I would like to complement Professor Pannell's excellent chapter with some observations on Massachusetts professional and non-professional education. First, I think that to a certain extent those figures are not comparable from state to state. For instance, professional and specialized expenditures are $55,000 to a student in

79

Connecticut, $2,300 in Maine, and $4,000 in Massachusetts. It is quite obvious to me that the high figure for Connecticut solely represents the medical and dental expenditures per student of the University of Connecticut. Maine does not have a medical or dental school, and therefore some other factor must be represented there, such as expenditures per teacher. In Massachusetts it may be something else, such as engineers and teachers.

It must be remembered that medical, dental, and veterinary schools are extremely expensive, and you really have to sort them out if you are going to look at the budget intelligently and compare the various states. As it happens, at Tufts we have done a fairly detailed analysis of this, and we find that in Connecticut the figure for medical and dental students is about $55,000 per student. In Massachusetts in the state medical school the figure is upwards of $60,000 per student. At Tufts we have what we think is a superior dental-medical education which costs on the order of $25,000 per student. Our schools are much larger, and my feeling is that we are much more economical. Connecticut just started the dental school at the very time when there is a surplus of dentists in New England. They are operating an extremely expensive school at $55,000 per student, and they have 40 to 50 students. They have done this at about the same time that we have decided to reduce our enrollment by forty students because of the saturation of dentists in New England, for which we have traditionally provided at least one half of the dentists.

This example illustrates the fact that there is now a considerable waste in resources in the public sector due to duplication in each state of what in fact should be devised for the economy of all New England. There is another way to provide, in effect, more money per student and improve the educational quality of the region. It may be impossible to do politically, but it is the only sensible way. It consists in looking at the needs of the region, and deciding what institutions we can do without. It is my contention that there are a number of institutions that we can do without, and that there are a number of situations where we could replace state institutions by scholarships to private institutions. We should hope that the New England Board of Higher Education could be the tool whereby these two types of measures could be planned.

I might point out another characteristic that has not been mentioned about New England: It is the only region I know of where, outside of the 1 percent of students from extremely wealthy families, there is no difference in average income between people attending public versus private institutions. Therefore the social difference between the two, which is very apparent in other regions, does not exist here. My view is that, if we have the courage to do it, we should look at both public and private institutions in deciding which institutions we should close down. We should put in the same box the private and public institutions and look at what each can do best, what needs to be done, and then do it most economically.

I think that unless we do this, both the private and public institutions in New England are going to feel poor constantly.

Robert W. Eisenmenger: Four Major Problems for Higher Education in New England

Professor McPherson carefully analyzes the diverse linkages between higher education and research and productivity and clearly demonstrates the very subtle and complex nature of these links. He shows how an educated labor force can enhance the nation's productivity and welfare. He also eloquently argues that our region should support national programs which help education in general, specifically those which provide access for poorer students. We should oppose, as a region, programs that shift to the states the responsibility for financial aid for higher education. We should also oppose federal programs that grant tuition tax credits and special tax incentives for research, which he considers to be very inefficient subsidies. As an economist, I agree with him on all those matters.

Professor Pannell presents statistics that clearly demonstrate that the New England states, with the important exception of Rhode Island, spend fewer dollars than the national average for each student enrolled in a public higher educational institution. She argues for a series of innovative but reasonable tactics to encourage more spending on public higher education, and I agree with her thoughts as well.

I would like to concentrate here upon a few suggestions as to how Pannell's and McPherson's somewhat generalized findings might be adapted to New England's unique situation. In my view New England has four major problems.

Shrinking Economic Resources

Problem number one is that New England is poor. Most of us who were brought up here don't think of New England as a poor region; it has a history of having well above average per capita income. Massachusetts and Connecticut, two of the most progressive states in the union, pioneered in all kinds of social legislation, educational assistance and training, and mental health and welfare programs. But the facts show that in the last 20 years the New England states, with the important exception of Connecticut, have become poor states. Per capita income figures show Connecticut to be substantially above the national average, and Massachusetts slightly above. But if you were to deflate those per capita income figures for the higher cost of living in New England, you would find that in fact each of the New England states except Connecticut has per capita income significantly below the national average. Maine is one of the poorest states in the union, if you deflate for the higher cost of living there.

In Table 3–3, Pannell presents data on New England state and local tax efforts. She shows that, relative to their economic base, Connecticut has a tax effort of 100 percent and Maine, 101 percent. These states spend more, or they sacrifice more, than the national average. The comparable figure for Massachusetts was 133 percent, for Rhode Island 114 percent, and for Vermont 106 percent, while the New Hampshire figure was only 73 percent. I think all those percentages are in fact higher. The actual sacrifice of real income for public programs is greater in New England than Pannell's figures show because the real cost of living is so much higher throughout New England. Consider Massachusetts, with 133 percent. I think it would be very hard indeed to encourage citizens of Massachusetts to sacrifice more. They are already sacrificing a lot for state and local programs. So if you are going to spend more for higher education, as Pannell advocates, then you are going to have less for something else.

Need for Advanced Skills

Problem number two is New England's ever-increasing dependence on a highly skilled labor force, which of course supports more spending for higher education. Historically New England's higher earnings were based on labor-intensive industries that required the special energies of an immigrant labor force. The textile, apparel, shoe and leather, jewelry, and paper industries all traditionally depended upon the working skills of a labor force brought in from all over the world, as well as from the declining farming areas in the northern tiers of the New England states.

Starting in 1920, however, immigration was substantially curtailed in this country. Over a period of three or four decades, this forced a movement out of low-skill labor-intensive industries into more highly skilled labor-intensive industries. The conversion took place at a cost of great personal agony for the many people who lost their jobs and couldn't find replacements. The situation was particularly difficult after World War II, when in the textile industry we lost an average of 1,000 jobs each month for almost a decade.

Now we are increasingly dependent on industries that require high skills of many kinds. The Massachusetts Division of Employment Security recently published a booklet titled "High Technology and Employment in Massachusetts" (April, 1981) that lists all the states according to their proportion of high technology industries in manufacturing. The first is New Hampshire, and Massachusetts is second. Vermont, surprisingly, is third, and Connecticut is fourth.

I think this ranking actually underestimates the degree of concentration in high technology industries in New England, because it deals just with manufacturing. Examples of the varied kinds of high technology industries we have in this region are abundant: the machine tool industry in Springfield, Vermont, Providence, Rhode Island, Worcester, Massachusetts, and Hartford, Connecticut; the razor blade industry in Boston and Connecticut; the medical instrumentation industry in Greater Boston; and the computer industry throughout New England. We also have the insurance industry in many locations throughout New England; the engineering and business consulting industries in Boston and Hartford; the aircraft and aircraft engine industry in Connecticut and in Lynn, Massachusetts; and the hospital industry, which has medical centers throughout New England. Because these medical centers attract many patients from outside the region, the hospital industry is really an export industry, much as our electronics industry is. And we have the private higher education industry throughout New England. In fact, the most important export industry in Massachusetts is private higher education.

All of these industries rely on a highly skilled labor force with a diversity of skills. If these high-skill industries are to be competitive in New England's harsh economic climate where a lot of the other inputs are high-priced, then they must have a plentiful supply of skilled labor at or below national average wage rates.

Furthermore, unless our secondary schools and institutions of higher education can produce these skills in abundance, I think the future of New England's economy is bleak. Fortunately in recent years the skilled labor force has been forthcoming, and New England's relative economic health is better than it has been for a decade. For about 20 years in the post-war period, Massachusetts, for example, had a declining relative per capita income. It went steadily down, I recall, from 12–13 percent above the national average to only 2 percent above the national average just a few years ago. In the last two or three years, however, it has gone back up to 105 percent of the national average.

Note that I emphasize the responsibility of institutions of higher education *and* the high schools. I think it a little presumptuous of those who have dealings with higher education to think economic success depends entirely on those institutions. Public institutions of higher education must produce the engineering and technical specialists as well as the liberal arts graduates needed for an increasingly labor-intensive industry in New England. Perhaps even more important, however, is the role of public high schools. Despite Professor Pannell's finding that we've spent a lot of money on secondary education in New England, the fact is that the level of education in public high schools in many of our larger cities has deteriorated steadily and rapidly. Unless high school students obtain basic training and conceptual skills they will be unable to continue their training, no matter how good and available higher education is. The lack of public concern about this problem troubles me. Smaller suburban towns have traditionally had a very high level of interest in maintaining the quality of secondary education, but there has been little public interest in sustaining even a minimum level of quality in city high schools in New England. And unless the high schools of Boston, Somerville, Fall River, New Bedford, and Worcester are doing their job, I'm not sure it will help to have the best public university system possible in Amherst. So that's New England's second problem: Its economy is uniquely dependent on a highly skilled labor force.

Lack of Commitment to Public Higher Education

Third, there is a conflict in New England between public and private education. There are at least two aspects to this conflict. One is primarily financial. As Tufts President Jean Mayer points out in his commentary, if Connecticut's public higher education system elects to put in a new dental school but New England needs only a limited number of dentists, Tufts is forced to cut back. Furthermore, if the new dental school is going to cost Connecticut $55,000 a head, it makes little sense. Thus there can be almost irreconcilable disagreement between public and private institutions. The public and private sectors in the Boston area provide another example: the University of Massachusetts' attempts to provide inexpensive high quality education conflict directly with the efforts of Boston College, Northeastern, Boston University, and the city's many other private schools.

Such tangible differences are only part of the problem. I suspect that an even more important source of conflict is the fact that most of the political leaders in New England, probably with the exception of Vermont and Rhode Island, have gone to private schools. You know we all have an irrational loyalty to the schools we attended. If you went to Harvard, you are loyal to that school. Since most political leaders in our states didn't go to the University of Massachusetts, they don't provide the support for the institutions of public higher education that you find in Wisconsin or California or Minnesota or Georgia. They just don't tend to consider public higher education as a very high priority item. Academic leaders in the public universities must demonstrate to political leaders who don't happen to have emotional attachments to their schools that the economy of the state and the region depends upon having a public higher educational system of extremely high quality.

The Creation of a Regional System

The fourth problem I will refer to is a vague one, yet it may be the most important element in my comments. It refers to something I call "rationalization" of the public higher educational systems in New England. Every educational institution must choose a principal mission or missions. Very few higher education systems can have multiple missions. Even the University of California at

Berkeley and Harvard University, two of the most elite of our institutions of higher education, cannot do everything well. It hasn't been clear to me that the public universities in New England have clearly defined their missions: What kind of students do they wish to attract? What specializations does each state wish to offer, so that it can have a rationalized system? In my view we should have a rationalized regional system, with centers of excellence in specific subject matter areas scattered throughout the region.

The New England Board of Higher Education has been trying for 30 years, with only modest success, to encourage the development of such centers of excellence at specific institutions throughout New England. Student grants should be transferable, so that a student from Maine could go to the University of Rhode Island and study oceanography, while a student from Massachusetts could study chemistry at the University of Maine. In fact, the provincial interests of state legislatures and the institutions themselves have generally discouraged this. As Pannell has clearly demonstrated, there now is a movement toward even more provincialism.

I think that there will also be a need in the future to be more specific about cost comparisons among public universities. It's not terribly helpful to say that we spend 20 percent less per student at the University of Massachusetts than at public universities in the nation unless we also compare the costs in Massachusetts of specific programs, such as engineering, with nationwide costs. University-wide figures can be misleading if most students happen to be specializing in business administration or English, very low-cost majors, as opposed to physics or engineering, which are very high-cost majors. If you standardize for the mix of the program output, cost differentials between New England and the nation may not be as large as Pannell suggests. Nevertheless, I wish to stress the need for the rationalization of public institutions of higher education and the need to eliminate overlapping and duplication, so that each institution can do a superior job in a few major fields rather than attempting to provide everything.

Chapter 5

HIGHER EDUCATION IN THE GROSS DOMESTIC PRODUCT OF THE NEW ENGLAND STATES

by Ward S. Curran

Education in general and higher education in particular have been viewed from several perspectives. One way to view education is as a source of training or, in economic terms, as a means through which an industrial society develops human capital. From a different perspective, we see education as the way in which the younger generation learns not only skills but also the history, literature, and culture of our society and of other societies.

Whatever we believe the role of higher education to be, it is an important sector of the economy. It is, in a word, an industry. Resources are employed to provide a set of services. The level of demand for these services may be a function of government funding, social custom, or law. This is particularly true at the elementary and secondary school levels.

The demand for higher education, however, may rest in part

Note: The author wishes to thank Dr. Melvin Bernstein of the New England Board of Higher Education for his helpful comments; Mr. Norman J. Brandt, Survey of the National Center for Education Statistics, U.S. Department of Education; Ms. Elizabeth Queen and Mr. Albert Silverman, U.S. Department of Commerce, Bureau of Economic Analysis; and Ms. Grace On and Ms. Sara Garian of the Federal Reserve Bank of Boston for their help in making data available to me to carry out this task.

upon its availability; that is, upon a tax-supported public university system. It may also rest upon the belief that the individual will benefit either in personal terms (a broadening of his or her intellectual horizons) or in terms of developing marketable skills (human capital), or both. In short, to think of higher education as a sector of the economy and, more specifically, as an industry, is to place it on a par with any service-oriented industry—medicine, for example. In this instance, however, a portion of the resources employed in the former are used to develop the human skills necessary to produce the latter.

The Importance of Higher Education in the New England Economy

One does not have to search far to find arguments for the importance of higher education—at least that portion of it devoted to scientific and technical training—to the future of the New England economy. As Browne and Hekman note:[1]

> *New England's educational system has a strong scientific orientation. The number of scientists and engineers who graduate from New England colleges and universities is greater than would be expected, based on the region's population. . . . The availability of such professionals clearly fosters the growth of industries with large research requirements. At the same time, the existence of a cluster of high technology firms attracts scientific and technical personnel because of the diversity of opportunities and greater employment security it offers.*

Although we recognize the nexus between higher education, technology, and the growth and development of a region or nation, we rarely discuss the size of the higher education industry relative to the output of goods and services it helps to generate. Indeed, on a state and regional basis the necessary data is not routinely published. Nevertheless, if we are to understand fully the contribution of higher education to the economy of a state or region, the size of the industry relative to output of all goods and services produced in that state or region is a useful starting point. Such a measure represents the direct rather than the indirect contribution of the industry to the economy of the state or region.

What follows, then, is an effort to establish the data base necessary to measure the direct contribution of higher education to the New England economy. It is the author's hope that what is presented here will lead to further refinements and subsequently to routine publication of the appropriate data.

The Relationship Between Gross Domestic Product and Current Fund Expenditures

The value of all goods and services produced in an economy is the gross domestic product (GDP) for that economy. For example, in 1979 the GDP of the United States was $2,370.1 billion.[2] The comparable figure for New England was a gross regional product of $123.7 billion or 5.2 percent of the GDP for the United States.[3]

A widely used measure of spending by institutions of higher education consists of the categories that comprise current fund expenditures. These expenditures include all of the educational and general expenditures associated with the academic function as well as those associated with auxiliary enterprises such as hospital services, and independent operations, including federally funded research and development centers.[4] In short, current fund expenditures are a comprehensive measure of the annual or, in most instances, fiscal year operating expenses of institutions of higher education.

Table 5–1 shows the proportion of gross domestic product accounted for by the New England states for the calendar year 1979

Table 5–1 Proportions of Gross Domestic Product and Current Fund Expenditures of Higher Education Accounted for by the New England States

State/Area	Gross Domestic Product (CY 1979)		Current Fund Expenditures (FY 1979)	
	Billions of Dollars	% of U.S. Total	Millions of Dollars	% of U.S. Total
Aggregate U.S.	2,370.1	100.0	51,051	100.0
New England	123.7	5.2	3,656	7.2
Conn.	36.5	1.6	717	1.4
Maine	8.3	0.3	186	0.4
Mass.	58.5	2.5	2,077	4.1
N.H.	7.8	0.3	235	0.5
R.I.	8.3	0.3	276	0.5
Vt.	4.0	0.2	165	0.3

SOURCES: *Survey of Current Business*, April 1981, p. 14; Federal Reserve Bank of Boston, *Gross State Product* New England; U.S. Office of Education partially edited data on Education and General Expenditures.

Table 5–2   Current Fund Expenditures of Institutions of Higher Education, by Type of Institutional Unit, for Fiscal Years 1979 and 1980 ($ thousands)

	FY 1979			FY 1980		
	All Institutions	Public	Private	All Institutions	Public	Private
Aggregate U.S.	51,052,222	33,961,249	17,090,973	57,117,049	37,931,086	19,185,963
New England	3,655,638	1,213,475	2,442,163	4,134,432	1,341,773	2,792,659
Conn.	716,936	298,487	418,449	808,149	334,497	473,653
Maine	185,650	121,234	64,416	209,710	138,278	71,431
Mass.	2,076,877	455,469	1,621,408	2,354,385	495,673	1,858,712
N.H.	234,985	111,540	123,445	258,184	119,368	138,816
R.I.	276,086	129,647	146,438	311,590	144,002	167,588
Vt.	165,104	97,097	68,007	192,414	109,954	82,460
Aggregate U.S.	100.0%	100.0%	100.0%	100.0%	100.0%	100.0%
New England (% of total)	7.2	3.6	14.3	7.2	3.5	14.6
Conn.	1.4	0.9	2.4	1.4	0.9	2.5
Maine	0.4	0.4	0.4	0.4	0.4	0.4
Mass.	4.1	1.3	9.5	4.1	1.3	9.7
N.H.	0.5	0.3	0.7	0.5	0.3	0.7
R.I.	0.5	0.4	0.9	0.5	0.4	0.9
Vt.	0.3	0.3	0.4	0.3	0.3	0.4

SOURCES: For fiscal 1979 see U.S. Department of Education, National Center for Education Statistics, *Financial Statistics of Institutions of Higher Education*, State Data, pp. 12–29. The data for fiscal 1980 are courtesy of the National Center for Education Statistics.

and the current fund expenditures of institutions of higher education for the fiscal year 1979. Massachusetts and Connecticut are
the major contributors to both totals. However, it is interesting
to note that while New England accounts for 5.2 percent of the
nation's gross domestic product, it accounts for 7.2 percent of the
current fund expenditures of institutions of higher education.
From the data it is apparent that the state of Massachusetts is the
source of the difference.

In Table 5–2 we have broken out the current fund expenditures
by type of institution (public or private) for the fiscal years 1979
and 1980. The data reveal that the private sector in fiscal 1979
accounted for 14.3 percent nationally of the private current fund
expenditures for institutions of higher education, with Massachusetts accounting for 9.5 percent of the total. In fiscal 1980 the
private sector accounted for 14.6 percent of the national total for
private colleges and universities. Massachusetts accounted for 9.7
percent of the total. Moreover, while the public sector tends to
dominate higher education nationally, in New England the private
sector, with the exception of Maine and Vermont, is the more
important component of these current fund expenditures. And
even in these two states, the public sector cannot be said to
dominate higher educational services.

Because current fund expenditures are generally reported on
a fiscal year basis and figures for the gross domestic product are
on a calendar year basis, it is necessary to average fiscal 1978 (not
shown in the table) with fiscal 1979 and fiscal 1979 with fiscal 1980
in order to approximate calendar year expenditures for 1979 and
1980. The results are shown in Table 5–3.

In Table 5–4 we have divided the current fund expenditures
of institutions of higher education by the gross domestic product
of the United States. We have repeated the process for New
England and for each of the New England states. The effort in
higher education in New England appears to be greater than it
is for the United States as a whole, with the private sector well
above the national average and the public sector below it. The
results in the public sector, however, are due to the relatively
low effort on the part of Connecticut and Massachusetts. All of
the other states are at or near the national average, and Vermont
is well above it. Within the private sector all of the New England
states except Maine are above the national average, while Maine
equals the national average.

Table 5–3   Current Fund Expenditures of Institutions of Higher Education for Calendar Years 1978 and 1979* ($ thousands)

	All Institutions	Publicly Controlled	Privately Controlled
	CY 1978)		
Aggregate U.S.	48,667,053	32,450,578	16,216,476
New England	3,469,709	1,150,099	2,319,610
Conn.	685,868	286,493	399,375
Maine	178,494	117,269	61,225
Mass.	1,958,854	421,473	1,537,381
N.H.	224,605	107,150	117,455
R.I.	262,996	124,315	138,681
Vt.	158,892	93,399	65,493
	CY 1979		
Aggregate U.S.	54,084,636	35,946,168	18,038,468
New England	3,895,035	1,277,624	2,617,411
Conn.	762,543	316,492	446,051
Maine	197,680	129,756	67,924
Mass.	2,215,631	475,571	1,740,060
N.H.	246,585	115,454	131,131
R.I.	293,838	136,825	157,013
Vt.	178,759	103,526	75,233

SOURCE: U.S. Department of Education, National Center for Education Statistics, *Financial Statistics of Institutions of Higher Education, State Data,* fiscal years 1978, 1979. The data for fiscal 1980 are courtesy of the National Center for Education Statistics.

* Calendar year 1978 equals one half of the sum of the expenditures for fiscal 1978 and fiscal 1979. Calendar year 1979 equals one half the sum of the expenditures for fiscal 1979 and fiscal 1980.

Developing a New Data Base

Although current fund expenditures of institutions of higher education are routinely collected and published, the same cannot be said for the data required to measure the direct contribution of higher education to the gross domestic product of the nation, region, or state. The value of all goods and services produced in the domestic economy is the sum of personal consumption expenditures, gross private domestic investment, and government expenditures on goods and services. In principle, the amount spent on higher education would be included in personal consumption expenditures (primarily tuition, fees, room and board). Investment in private higher education would be included in gross

Table 5–4   Current Fund Expenditures for Institutions of Higher Education as a Percentage of Gross Domestic Product for 1978 and 1979

	Percentage of 1978 GDP		
	All Institutions	*Publicly Controlled*	*Privately Controlled*
United States	2.3	1.5	0.8
New England	3.1	1.0	2.1
Conn.	2.1	0.9	1.2
Maine	2.4	1.6	0.8
Mass.	3.7	0.8	2.9
N.H.	3.3	1.6	1.7
R.I.	3.4	1.6	1.8
Vt.	4.4	2.5	1.9
	Percentage of 1979 GDP		
United States	2.3	1.5	0.8
New England	3.1	1.0	2.1
Conn.	2.1	0.9	1.2
Maine	2.4	1.6	0.8
Mass.	3.7	0.8	2.9
N.H.	3.2	1.5	1.7
R.I.	3.5	1.7	1.8
Vt.	4.5	2.5	2.0

SOURCE: See Tables 5–1, 5–2, and 5–3. The GDP for 1978 was $2,107 billion. See U.S. Department of Commerce *Survey of Current Business*, April 1980, p. 14.

private domestic investment. In the government sector would be all current expenditures as well as capital spent on higher education.

Alternatively, the private sector's contribution to higher education could be added to government expenditures. The procedure is straightforward. It was first suggested by Kendrick and Jaycox[5] and is currently employed by the Federal Reserve Bank of Boston in estimating the gross regional product and gross state products in New England.

In either approach we must include government expenditures on higher education. When using the Kendrick-Jaycox technique, however, the contribution of the private sector is developed from data on wages and salaries. We shall illustrate both approaches, beginning with direct expenditures on goods and services. A major if imperfect source from which to develop the data is the annual publication of the U.S. Department of Education's National Cen-

ter for Education Statistics, *Financial Statistics of Institutions of
Higher Education State Data.* This publication includes both current fund revenues and expenditures as well as changes in plant
and equipment.

The source is imperfect because, first, it may not accurately
account for new investment expenditures in higher education. For
example, a gift to build a new laboratory might be included under
gifts and grants and the entire expenditure charged to an account
in educational and general expenditures. Alternatively, the school
could borrow money (a liability) and build the laboratory (an asset).
Amortization of principle along with interest on the loan will be
captured in current fund expenditures over several years, yet the
investment—the new laboratory—is properly included in the gross
domestic product for the year in which it was built.

Second, payments for services rendered are often lumped together with transfer payments. For example, a government or
private agency may purchase a service from a university, perhaps
a research project. This payment is properly included in the gross
domestic product. Alternatively, the agency may give money to
be used for scholarships. This is a transfer payment and not properly included in the gross domestic product.

Finally, the data employed is on a fiscal year, not a calendar
year, basis. To make it comparable with data on the gross domestic
product, simply average the two fiscal years that circumscribe a
calendar year. The average of the data for fiscal years 1979 and
1980, for example, will be treated as if it were data for the calendar
year 1979. Since not all educational institutions and government
agencies end their fiscal years on June 30, the actual expenditures
for the calendar year may vary somewhat from the fiscal year
averages.

At the level of detail currently available, isolating investment
expenditures is difficult. Changes in the plant account from year
to year may necessarily reflect more than new investment. Even
to the extent that such changes do reflect new investment, they
cannot be added to data from current fund revenues and expenditures without running some risk of double-counting. Although we may err on the side of understating actual investment
expenditures, we shall not include net additions to the plant account in our calculations.

Again, because of insufficient detail in the published data, we
cannot completely separate payments for services rendered from
transfers. To circumvent the problem we shall first err on the side

of understatement by excluding all gifts, grants, and contracts. Then we shall err on the side of overstating the contribution of higher education to gross domestic product by including these categories in our computations.

Under current reporting procedures there are six categories of current fund revenue that would reflect payment for goods and services produced by higher education. (These are listed in Table 5–5 for fiscal years 1979 and 1980.) Five of these—tuition and

Table 5–5   Current Fund Revenues of Institutions of Higher Education in
FY 1979 and 1980, Aggregate United States and New England
($ thousands)

	FY 1979			
	Aggregate U.S.	% of Total	New England	% of Total
Total	40,715,895	100.0	2,628,290	100.0
Tuition and fees	10,807,210	26.5	1,222,070	46.5
Government appropriations	18,368,086	45.1	630,391	24.0
Endowment income	986,093	2.4	186,192	7.1
Sales of educational services	1,039,653	2.6	53,571	2.0
Sales and services of auxiliary enterprises	5,751,400	14.1	476,959	18.1
Sales and services of hospitals	3,763,453	9.2	59,107	2.2
	FY 1980			
Total	45,454,396	100.0	2,930,244	100.0
Tuition and fees	12,029,839	26.5	1,377,556	47.0
Government appropriations	20,296,971	44.7	703,722	24.0
Endowment income	1,160,210	2.6	210,360	7.2
Sales of educational services	1,237,265	2.7	66,273	2.3
Sales and services of auxiliary enterprises	6,430,846	14.1	542,425	18.5
Sales and services of hospitals	4,299,265	9.5	29,908	1.0

SOURCE: For fiscal 1979, see U.S. Department of Education, National Center for Education Statistics, *Financial Statistics of Institutions of Higher Education, Fiscal Year 1979*, pp. 12–17. Data for fiscal 1980 is preliminary and courtesy of the National Center for Education Statistics.

fees, government appropriations, sales of educational services, and
sales and services of auxiliary enterprises and hospitals—represent
direct payments. The sixth, endowment income, is included because it helps to cover the expenses of providing these services.
Moreover, since wages and salaries are the primary cost of funding
higher education and since the alternative technique for measuring
the contribution of an industry to the GDP is built upon wages
and salaries, exclusion of endowment income would understate
the value of the goods and services produced. Thus endowment
income is generally not used for transfer payments such as scholarships (although in some private institutions a small part of en-

Table 5–6   Gross Domestic Product Originating in Institutions of Higher Ed-
            ucation Based on Current Fund Revenues, Calendar Years 1978
            and 1979 ($ millions)

	CY 1978		
	Total Revenues*	GDP	% of Total
Aggregate U.S.	38,945	2,127,000	1.8
New England	2,505	111,194	2.3
Conn.	514	32,831	1.6
Maine	145	7,466	1.9
Mass.	1,337	52,878	2.5
N.H.	168	6,844	2.5
R.I.	213	7,538	2.8
Vt.	128	3,604	3.6
	CY 1979		
Aggregate U.S.	43,085	2,370,100	1.8
New England	2,779	123,685	2.2
Conn.	563	36,810	1.5
Maine	155	8,256	1.9
Mass.	1,492	58,546	2.5
N.H.	179	7,765	2.3
R.I.	239	8,262	2.9
Vt.	139	4,026	3.5

SOURCE: U.S. Department of Education, National Center for Education Statistics, *Financial
Statistics of Institutions of Higher Education, Fiscal Year 1979*, pp. 12–29. Federal Reserve
Bank of Boston, Gross State Product New England. Data for fiscal 1980 and calendar year
1979 are courtesy of the National Center for Education Statistics and the Federal Reserve
Bank of Boston.

* Includes tuition and fees, endowment income, government appropriations, sales of educational activities, sales and services of auxiliary enterprises, and sales and services of
hospitals. Data is the average of fiscal years.

dowment income may be specifically designated for scholarships). Rather, it represents a subsidy that helps to defray the costs of the services provided.

By averaging FY 1978 (now shown) with FY 1979 and FY 1979 with FY 1980, and then dividing the results by the gross domestic product, we can calculate the importance of higher education to the gross domestic product of the United States and the New England states (see Table 5–6). As calculated in every New England state except Connecticut, higher education accounts for a larger percentage of the GDP than it does for the United States as a whole. If we add two additional categories, government contracts and grants and private contracts, gifts, and grants (see Table 5–7), and repeat the calculations, the comparative role of higher education in the gross domestic product of New England relative to that of the United States is even higher. (See Table 5–8.)

Bearing in mind that the former calculations may understate and the latter overstate the direct contribution of higher education to the gross domestic product of the nation and the region, we

Table 5–7   Government Grants and Private Grants and Contracts, Aggregate United States and New England States, Fiscal 1979 and 1980 ($ thousands)

| | FY 1979 | | | |
	Aggregate U.S.	% of Total	New England	% of Total
Total current fund revenues	52,184,608	100.0	3,728,228	100.0
Government contracts and grants	6,631,060	12.7	604,473	16.2
Private contracts and grants	2,491,193	4.8	259,405	7.0
	FY 1980			
Total current fund revenues	58,691,300	100.0	4,216,035	100.0
Government contracts and grants	7,604,180	13.0	709,280	16.8
Private contracts and grants	2,833,861	4.8	301,118	7.1

SOURCE: U.S. Department of Education, National Center for Education Statistics, *Financial Statistics of Institutions of Higher Education, Fiscal Year 1979*, pp. 12–17. Data for fiscal year 1980 is preliminary and courtesy of the National Center for Education Statistics.

Table 5-8   Gross Domestic Product Originating in Institutions of Higher Education, Based on Current Fund Revenues for Calendar Years 1978 and 1979 ($ millions)

	CY 1978		
	*Total Revenues**	*Gross Domestic Product*	*% of Total*
Aggregate U.S.	47,615	2,127,000	2.2
New England	3,320	111,194	3.0
Conn.	670	32,831	2.0
Maine	177	7,466	2.4
Mass.	1,852	52,878	3.5
N.H.	205	6,849	3.0
R.I.	259	7,538	3.4
Vt.	157	3,604	4.4
	CY 1979		
Aggregate U.S.	52,865	2,370,100	2.2
New England	3,716	123,685	3.0
Conn.	740	36,810	2.0
Maine	190	8,256	2.3
Mass.	2,081	58,546	3.6
N.H.	225	7,765	2.9
R.I.	276	8,262	3.3
Vt.	170	4,026	4.2

Source: U.S. Department of Education, National Center for Education Statistics, *Financial Statistics of Institutions of Higher Education, Fiscal Year 1979*, pp. 12–17. Data for fiscal year 1980 is preliminary and courtesy of the National Center for Education Statistics.

* Includes tuition and fees, endowment income, government appropriations, sales of educational activities, sales and services of auxiliary enterprises, sales and services of hospitals, government grants and contracts, and private gifts, grants, and contracts.

can tentatively conclude that higher education currently accounts for about 2 percent of the gross domestic product of the United States. In New England probably more than 2.5 percent but less than 3 percent of the gross regional product is attributable to higher education. In four of the six New England states the contribution may exceed 3 percent, and in the case of Vermont approximately 4 percent, of the gross state product. Maine is near the national average and Connecticut is slightly below it.

The Kendrick-Jaycox Technique

To implement this approach we begin with the personal income data for states, which is collected by the U.S. Department of

Commerce. To obtain what is technically known as *National Income* (NI), profit or profit-type income (a surplus of revenues over expenses) and net income are added to employee compensation in any particular industry. Then to national income we add indirect business taxes, such as sales and excise taxes, which have been included in the costs of production (that is, have been added to the interest) and profits. The result is technically known as the Net National Product (NNP). Capital consumption allowances consisting largely but not exclusively of depreciation on plant and equipment are added to the net national product to obtain the contribution of the industry to the gross domestic product.[6]

On the state level, personal income data is readily available.[7] Moreover, it is broken out by industry. Under the Standard Industrial Classification scheme employed by the U.S. Department of Commerce, however, data is aggregated in the service industries only at the two-digit level. Thus Standard Industrial Classification 82 is "Educational Services." Colleges, universities, professional schools, junior colleges, and technical institutes constitute the subset SIC 822. Furthermore, since higher education is broken out into a public as well as a private sector, the former enters into the gross domestic product through government expenditures on goods and services.

We can illustrate the Kendrick-Jaycox approach with SIC 82 and then adapt it to SIC 822. Using the 1978 data[8] at the national level for SIC 82, Educational Services, we have the figures shown in the table.

	$ millions
Wages and salaries	$12,255
Other compensation	4
Profit-type income	528
Net interest	−1
National Income	12,786
Indirect business taxes	123
Net National Product	12,909
Capital consumption allowance	131
Gross product originating in SIC 82	13,040

Thus for the United States, private educational services accounted for $13,040 million, or about 0.6 percent of the 1978 GDP of $2,127.6 billion.

The critical assumption in the Kendrick-Jaycox technique is that the structure of each industry within the state is the same as that for the nation or that differences are offsetting. Based on this assumption, we can follow the procedure as illustrated in Figure 5–1 and estimate the gross product originating in each state from

Figure 5–1   Estimating the Gross State Product

(1) *Private Non-Farm*

We can "blow-up" the available components of product (from state personal income series) to total industry product by using national coefficients.

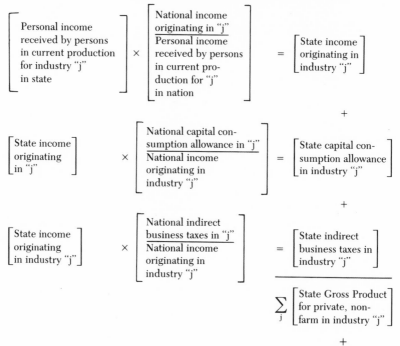

$$\left[\begin{array}{l}\text{Personal income}\\\text{received by persons}\\\text{in current production}\\\text{for industry "j"}\\\text{in state}\end{array}\right] \times \left[\begin{array}{l}\text{National income}\\\text{originating in "j"}\\\hline\text{Personal income}\\\text{received by persons}\\\text{in current pro-}\\\text{duction for "j"}\\\text{in nation}\end{array}\right] = \left[\begin{array}{l}\text{State income}\\\text{originating in}\\\text{industry "j"}\end{array}\right]$$

$+$

$$\left[\begin{array}{l}\text{State income}\\\text{originating}\\\text{in "j"}\end{array}\right] \times \left[\begin{array}{l}\text{National capital con-}\\\text{sumption allowance in "j"}\\\hline\text{National income}\\\text{originating in}\\\text{industry "j"}\end{array}\right] = \left[\begin{array}{l}\text{State capital con-}\\\text{sumption allowance}\\\text{in industry "j"}\end{array}\right]$$

$+$

$$\left[\begin{array}{l}\text{State income}\\\text{originating}\\\text{in industry "j"}\end{array}\right] \times \left[\begin{array}{l}\text{National indirect}\\\text{business taxes in "j"}\\\hline\text{National income}\\\text{originating in}\\\text{industry "j"}\end{array}\right] = \left[\begin{array}{l}\text{State indirect}\\\text{business taxes in}\\\text{industry "j"}\end{array}\right]$$

$$\sum_{j}\left[\begin{array}{l}\text{State Gross Product}\\\text{for private, non-}\\\text{farm in industry "j"}\end{array}\right]$$

$+$

(2) *Farm (from Department of Agriculture)*   State Gross Farm Product

$+$

(3) *Government (from Department of Commerce)*   Government State Product

The procedure of blowing-up state personal income in the *private non-farm* industries assumes that the structure of each industry within the state is the same as that for the nation, or that the differences are offsetting. This assumption is likely not to hold up for smaller states and SMSAs. Even for the larger, more economically integrated states and SMSAs, the validity of this assumption may be questioned.

SOURCE: Grace On, *Gross State Product New England*, Boston: Federal Reserve Bank of Boston, 1981. See also John W. Kendrick and C. Milton Jaycox, "The Concept and Estimation of Gross State Product," *Southern Economic Journal*, vol. 32, no. 2 (October 1965), pp. 163–168.

private educational services. In Connecticut, for example, wages and salaries for 1978 were $351,508 million.

$$\$351,508 \times \frac{12,786}{12,255} = \$366,739$$

$$\$366,739 \times \frac{131}{12,786} = 3,757$$

$$\$366,739 \times \frac{123}{12,786} = 3,528$$

$$\overline{\$374,024}$$

The calculations can be further simplified by multiplying wages and salaries for the state by the ratio of gross national product originating in this sector to wages and salaries for that sector. Again, for Connecticut:

$$\$351,508 \times \frac{13,040}{12,255} = \$374,024$$

To apply this approach to SIC 822 is more difficult. Since the Department of Commerce has to date refined the data base only to the two-digit level, we must make certain "heroic" assumptions using the available data. In recent years for both the public and private sectors the U. S. Department of Commerce has made available state data on wages and salaries of college and university employees covered under the state unemployment insurance programs. For the private sector we multiply this data by a factor representing the national ratio of uncovered to covered employees in the system. On the assumption that what is true of SIC 82 is true of SIC 822, we multiply the adjusted wage and salary figure by the ratio of gross product originating in SIC 82 to wages and salaries in SIC 82 to obtain an estimate of the gross product originating in SIC 822. For the public sector we multiply wages and salaries by the national ratio of appropriations in the public sector for SIC 822 to wages and salaries for SIC 822. All ratios for the years 1978 and 1979 are shown in Table 5–9.

To implement this approach, we shall employ the wage and salary data for the New England states, multiplying by the national ratios and dividing by the gross domestic product for the state. Thus for Connecticut, for 1978, we have:

Table 5–9   Wages and Salaries in SIC 822, Gross Product Originating in SIC 82, and Government Appropriations in SIC 822 Public Sector, for the United States in 1978 and 1979 ($ millions)

	(1) *Adjusted Wages* *and Salaries* *SIC 822*	*(2)* *Wages and* *Salaries* *SIC 822*	*(3)* *Ratio of* *(1) to (2)*
1978	$6,972	$6,665	1.05
1979	$7,588	$7,203	1.05

	(4) *Gross Product* *Originating* *in SIC 82*	*(5)* *Wages and* *Salaries* *SIC 82*	*(6)* *Ratio of* *(4) to (5)*
1978	$13,040	$12,255	1.06
1979	$14,366	$13,523	1.06

	(7) *Government* *Appropriations* *to SIC 822* *Public Sector*	*(8)* *Wages and* *Salaries* *SIC 822* *Public Sector*	*(9)* *Ratio of* *(7) to (8)*
1978	$17,268	$16,312	1.06
1979	$18,935	$17,819	1.06

SOURCES: U.S. Department of Commerce, unpublished data. For government appropriations see U.S. Department of Education, National Center for Education Statistics, *Financial Statistics of Institutions of Higher Education*, fiscal years 1978, 1979. Data for 1978 and 1979 are averages of fiscal 1978 and 1979 and fiscal 1979 and 1980. Data for fiscal 1980 are courtesy of National Center for Education Statistics.

Wages and Salaries
SIC 822
Private Sector
(millions of dollars)

$$\$195 \times 1.05 = 205$$
$$\$205 \times 1.06 = 217$$

Wages and Salaries
SIC 822
Public Sector
(millions of dollars)

$$\$151 \times 1.06 = 160$$

Private	*Public*	*Total*
$\dfrac{217}{32,831} = 0.7\%$	$\dfrac{160}{32,831} = 0.5\%$	$\dfrac{377}{32,831} = 1.2\%$

The results of similar computations are shown in Table 5–10 for the United States and the six New England states.

Table 5–10   Percentage of Domestic Product Accounted for by Higher Education in United States and New England, 1978 and 1979

	1978		
	Public	*Private*	*Total*
U.S.	0.8%	0.4%	1.2%
New England	0.5	1.1	1.6
Conn.	0.5	0.7	1.2
Maine	0.8	0.3	1.1
Mass.	0.5	1.4	1.9
N.H.	0.9	0.7	1.6
R.I.	1.0	0.9	1.9
Vt.	1.3	0.8	2.1
	1979		
U.S.	0.8%	0.3%	1.2%
New England	0.5	1.0	1.4
Conn.	0.5	0.6	1.1
Maine	0.8	0.4	1.2
Mass.	0.4	1.4	1.8
N.H.	0.7	0.8	1.5
R.I.	0.9	1.0	1.9
Vt.	1.2	0.8	2.0

SOURCES: U.S. Department of Commerce, unpublished data. For government appropriations see U.S. Department of Education, National Center for Education Statistics, *Financial Statistics of Institutions of Higher Education*, fiscal years 1978, 1979. Data for 1978 and 1979 are averages of fiscal 1978 and 1979 and fiscal 1979 and 1980. Data for fiscal 1980 are courtesy of National Center for Education Statistics.

In nearly all cases the percentage of gross domestic product accounted for by SIC 822 is less than 2 percent and often closer to 1 percent. The results appear to be lower than what was obtained when we attempted the direct approach. Of course, the "heroic" assumptions may not hold in practice. For example, in some of the New England states, particularly Vermont and New Hampshire, tuition and fees play a larger role than government appropriations in funding expenditures and hence in contributing to wages and salaries in SIC 822.[9] To assume, as our calculations do, that government appropriations alone will account for the difference between wages and salaries and total expenditures on public higher education is not consistent with the facts for many states.

In general, of course, to assume (as does the Kendrick-Jaycox approach) that what is true of the United States is also true of the

Table 5–11   **Percentage of Total Wages and Salaries Accounted for by Higher Education in the United States and New England, 1976–1980**

Year	U.S.	N.E.	Conn.	Maine	Mass.	N.H.	R.I.	Vt.
1976	1.8%	2.7%	1.9%	1.7%	3.2%	2.7%	2.8%	3.4%
1977	1.7	2.5	1.8	1.7	2.9	2.4	2.7	3.4
1978	1.8	2.3	1.7	1.6	2.8	2.3	2.7	3.0
1979	1.7	2.2	1.5	1.6	2.6	2.1	2.6	2.9
1980	1.7	2.1	1.6	1.6	2.5	2.1	2.6	3.1

SOURCES: Data on personal income and total wages, salaries and proprietor's income can be found in *Survey of Current Business*, Vol. 1, July 1981, pp. 32–37. Wages and salaries for SIC 822 are courtesy of the U.S. Department of Commerce, Regional Economic Measurement Division, with permission from the six New England states to use the data. The full tables reported on in this chapter are available from the author by request.

individual states may also be inaccurate, particularly as one tries to break down industries into subsets. To partially circumvent this difficulty, compare wages and salaries in SIC 822 for the public and private sectors with wages and salaries for the United States and New England. Here we need only rely on one "heroic" assumption; specifically, that the ratio of adjusted wages and salaries in SIC 822 to total wages and salaries for SIC 822 for the United States is the same for each of the New England states. The results for comparable data from 1975 to 1980 are shown in Table 5–11. For New England, over 2 percent of all wages and salaries and proprietor's income generated in the region are attributable to employment in some capacity in higher education while the national average is under 2 percent. Of the six New England states, Massachusetts, New Hampshire, Rhode Island, and Vermont exceed the national average; Connecticut and Maine are near it.

Summary

From the data currently available one can only crudely estimate the direct contribution of higher education to the gross domestic products of the New England states. The data do suggest, however, that for the United States as a whole higher education accounts for 1 to 2 percent of the gross domestic product. For New England, higher education plays an even larger role. It is especially significant in Massachusetts, where the private sector makes a large contribution. Within the economies of the three smaller New England states—Vermont, New Hampshire, and Rhode Island—higher education is relatively more important than it is for the nation as a whole.

The above generalization may be extended or modified as further research yields a more refined data base, which in turn can be easily placed on computer tapes. When this is accomplished, researchers and policy-makers will be in a better position to compare the importance of higher education with other industries within the economies of the New England states.[10] Policy-makers will then have a more complete understanding of the direct impact that changes in expenditures in this sector will have on the overall economic health and vitality of the region.

Endnotes

1. Lynn E. Browne and John S. Hekman, "New England's Economy in the 1980's," *New England Economic Review*, January-February 1981, p. 11.
2. The more familiar GNP for the United States was $2,413.9 billion. The difference of $43.1 billion is attributable to the foreign section, that is, exports less imports. See U.S. Department of Commerce, *Survey of Current Business*, April 1981, p. 14.
3. Courtesy of the Federal Reserve Bank of Boston.
4. U.S. Department of Education, *1980 Digest of Education Statistics*, p. 152.
5. John W. Kendrick and C. Milton Jaycox, "The Concept and Estimation of Gross State Product," *Southern Economic Journal*, Vol. 32, No. 2 (October 1965), pp. 153–68.
6. We have limited our discussion here to those details pertinent to education. For a more complete discussion of national income accounting see U.S. Department of Commerce, Bureau of Economic Analysis, "The National Income and Product Accounts of the United States 1929–1980: An Introduction to Revised Estimate," *Survey of Current Business*, December 1980.
7. Regional Economic Measurement Division, "Revised State Personal Income 1969–1980," *Survey of Current Business*, July 1981, pp. 29–72.
8. Data courtesy of the Department of Commerce, Regional Economic Analysis, Regional Economic Systems.
9. National Center for Education Statistics, *The Condition of Education*, 1980 edition (Washington, D.C.: U.S. Government Printing Office), pp. 1954–57.
10. Industries including higher education are, of course, compared on the basis of employment. See New England Regional Commission, *The New England Regional Plan: An Economic Development Strategy* (Boston: New England Regional Commission, 1980). To compare industries on the basis of aggregate expenditures, however, is to recognize the impact of the industry on the total output of goods and services rather than simply on the level of employment.

Chapter 6

COOPERATION FOR WHAT?

by Anthony P. Carnevale

The topic of education-business relations always revolves around the same theme—how to cooperate more effectively. The tone of conferences held to pursue this theme is remarkably similar— barely disguised frustration. Both educators and corporate representatives seem to feel that the other is intending a raid on traditional institutional prerogatives. As a result, much valuable time and emotional energy is wasted in defensive reaction.

Many begin with the presumption that successful cooperation between education and business is new and uncharted territory. In truth, they have been cooperating vigorously and successfully since the United States became the world's educational-industrial bellwether in the late 1940s. The vigorous demands of war production and military mobilization are early examples of the fundamental flexibility of our educational and private enterprise institutions. Upon demobilization in the late forties, the educators' contribution in transforming an agrarian population into a managerial and technical pool accounted for no small part of our remarkable post-war economic boom and the subsequent "golden age of American productivity." Together education and enterprise attained the scientific and production know-how that outdistanced our Soviet cousins rather easily after the first space shot was fired in the 1950s. Together they dramatically increased educational achievement and reduced poverty by two thirds after we discovered those "other Americans" in the early 1960s.

So, if the romance between education and enterprise has been such a successful entanglement, why hasn't the relationship settled into a blissful union? Perhaps it is in the best interests of all parties for this middle-aged liaison to end. The baby boom is over—the children are grown—and there no longer seems any practical purpose to the marriage. This brings me back to my beginning. The hard question that often goes begging and, in my view, the source of mutual frustration is: *Cooperation for what?*

Until we decide *why* education and enterprise need to renew cooperative arrangements, discussion of the issue will wander aimlessly between the defensive embattlements of each set of institutions. I will leave the methods, modes, and mechanisms for cooperation to educators and corporate executives. For my part, I will take a whack at the "for what?"

Let me begin by asserting that cooperation is more necessary than ever before. The conditions for cooperation have changed, but not its fundamental importance. Fortunately or unfortunately, the new imperatives for cooperation are unannounced by what theoreticians call "action-forming events": There are no attacks on Pearl Harbor; no Sputnik; and as yet no latter-day Michael Harrington to signal a common starting point or common ground for cooperation. Instead, the new bases for cooperation are the stuff of deliberate trends that comfort us with their deadening regularity: declining productivity, declining real wages, declining competitive advantage in world markets, accelerating rates of interest, inflation, the "necessary rate of unemployment at full employment," and the aging of the work force.

Our inability to react decisively to these trends is also the stuff of human nature. It is only human to ignore what lies over the next hill in favor of more proximate concerns. Even Lord Keynes, the granddaddy of twentieth-century economic planners, liked to ignore the long term. When asked to account for the distant implications of economic trends in his own day he replied, "In the long term we'll all be dead."

Keynes is dead and these same economic trends persist. The long term has arrived.

It is also human nature to waste that which is plentiful and ignore the consequences. For some time we have both enjoyed and struggled with a substantial labor surplus. The future promises a reduced and older work force.

It is the arrival of these fundamental economic and demographic trends that signals a new era for cooperation between education and industry. I would like to review some of the economic and demographic changes that afflict us and suggest some tentative education and training "strategies" in response. You should note that I speak of "strategies," not policies. The difference, I think, is more than semantic. Policy implies public. In my view public responses are only a piece of the puzzle. In fact, given the organization of the American social system into public and private sectors and given the size of the task at hand, public programs are likely to continue as the less important component. I use the word "strategy" to imply both public and private responses.

It is also my bias that enhancing American competitive advantage is very much in the public interest. However, while that which is in the "public interest" is naturally of public concern, it does not necessarily require public responsibility or public solutions. Moreover, even where public solutions are logical and efficient, it is my view that we should opt for the policies that require a minimum of public intervention into the private sphere. I would, for instance, prefer tax incentives over appropriated bureaucratic structures in response to public problems.

With the latter caveats in mind, let me turn to a discussion of the economic and demographic trends that will determine our future options and conclude with a survey of some guidelines and mechanisms for future education and training strategies. I will begin with a thumbnail sketch of the economic trends that have already overtaken us.

The Economic Trend

By 1941 the United States was a major military power. The Second World War unleashed our economic potential and gradually gave birth to a new social optimism based on our economic success. The hothouse economy of the post-war boom made it seem that we could produce abundance on such a scale that social problems would drown in a sea of resources. Social conflict, and the ideologies that fed upon it, would be abolished forever. By all reports, our principal problem as we ran pell-mell toward the post-industrial society was how to provide meaningful leisure.

Without repeating the familiar litany of decline, suffice it to say that things have changed for the worse since the 1940s. What's more important is that the decline in American productivity and competitive advantage couldn't have come at a worse time. Simply put, the pace for economic competition is accelerating and we are having some difficulty holding our own. Our economy is increasingly internationalized as we face serious challenges from other "more developed countries" (MDCs) and as "less developed countries" (LDCs) are utilizing their natural resources and large pools of unskilled labor to take their first steps up the economic development ladder.

This process is usually referred to as "rationalization" by economists. It is the root cause of our current economic malaise and the underlying economic process that will force profound changes in our economic and human resources strategies in the future. Economic rationalization is the process by which relatively higher technology, higher wage, higher productivity enterprise sorts itself out among the MDCs and, correspondingly, the process by which lower wage–lower productivity businesses settle in LDCs. The competitive advantage of the LDCs begins with their low-wage labor pool. Our own competitive advantage relies on the application of technological advances and our ability to maintain and accelerate the general skill level of our labor force.

In the long term we cannot protect our share of unskilled production. Ultimately we cannot match sweat equity with 950 million Chinese. Our real competitors are the other "more developed countries."

As the pace of technological change accelerates, our ability to *adapt* our human skills to the new technologies and to *integrate* new production techniques with available labor will be critical. Adaptation will be all the more difficult as product life and skill life become shorter and shorter. Moreover, it is ultimately the *rate* at which we apply new technologies and integrate them with a ready labor force that will determine our success. You should be warned that a return to the Golden Age of American Productivity will not be good enough. Our competitors have already far exceeded our best historical rates of productivity.

Our traditional economic strategies are no longer sufficient. More and more liberal and conservative analysts and policy-makers connect our poor overall economic performance to outworn economic strategies. Increasingly, for instance, liberal and conservative economists agree that our traditional manipulations of the overall level of spending and money supply have less and less positive impact on real growth, prices, productivity, and employment. Explanations for the failure of traditional macroeconomic policy vary, but analysts agree that persistent and indiscriminate restraint in the form of tight money and high interest rates eventually results in economic stagnancy, harming the long-term health of the economy. At the same time, a persistent and indiscriminate stimulus in the form of increased spending and easy money eventually results in inflation. As a result, policy-makers face an exasperating dilemma that does not allow either aggressive restraint or stimulus. Many economists now contend that we can escape the current dilemma only by reducing our reliance on traditional policies, complementing them with what are variously called "supply side" strategies by some and "structural" strategies by others. A suggested "human capital" strategy is generally among those recommended "supply side" or "structural" alternatives.

Defining a Human Capital Strategy

In simplest terms, a human capital strategy means more and better education and training. By education, I mean learning from the inside out: internalizing a fundamental understanding of the principles that govern a subject area. By training, I mean learning from the outside in: gaining a practical, job-specific capacity for performing tasks. These notions do not divide neatly by subject area or purpose. One can be trained or educated as an engineer, a chemist, an economist.

In addition, one needn't be educated in a subject area to be trained in it. A pilot needn't fully understand the aerodynamic principles behind aircraft design to fly a plane, nor must an engineer be able to pilot an airplane in order to build a better one. Finally, all subjects are suitable for both education and training. We have all learned lately that there is art even in motorcycle maintenance.

Both more education and more training will increase our productivity. On the one hand, education provides us with profound shifts in production methods, product lines, and technology. Training, on the other hand, leads to "process improvement," which incidentally accounts for the major share of productivity improvements in recent economic memory.

Another caveat: More is not necessarily better. Unless we define an increased capacity for education and training in the context of some general notions as to eventual goals we will waste our resources and ultimately fail in our purpose. In short, we need a strategy. By strategy I mean some loosely agreed upon recognition of what our problems are and how we might try to solve them. We need some common context in which we can all proceed separately without doing violence to the ultimate purposes and goals of individual public and private institutions. At a minimum, we need a good deal more information and a common language that communicates the new economic imperatives and allows us to consider our mutual possibilities.

The Case for a Human Capital Strategy

We will also need a shift in perspective where the importance of the human factor in production is concerned. A human capital strategy would represent a dramatic break with past practices. Unlike other industrialized nations, the United States has paid little attention to the role of human capital in the nation's economic adaptability, productivity, and competitive advantage. Government policies, especially federal education, employment, and training policies, evolved as arbiters of social equity and not for the promotion of human capital development or economic efficiency. At the same time, the $40 billion private training effort has been largely ignored by economic analysts and excluded from public debate over appropriate education and training strategies. Such practices were appropriate to an era of effortless growth. They are no longer appropriate to a new economic era of intense international economic competition, rapid technological change, and demographic shifts that will make workers scarce and non-workers plentiful.

The macroeconomic case for human capital is convincing. According to one interpretation of the available research on economic growth, between 1948 and 1979 human capital improvements accounted for a larger share of productivity growth than machine capital. In any event, there is no apparent rationale for public investment incentives that so dramatically favor machines over human capital. There are also private disincentives to human capital investment. In the private sector it is often the case that one employer invests in training and another in wages to bid away trained personnel. The overall effect of our public and private incentives is a national underinvestment in human capital.

The evidence that we have ignored and continue to ignore the economic importance of human capital is compelling. One striking bit of evidence is the dramatic rise in corporate expense for educational remediation and training. While remediation continues to represent an insignificant portion of private training, its spreading claim on private resources is alarming. Recently, the Conference Board reported that 37 percent of the firms it studies now provide remedial training in reading, writing, and arithmetic.

More general evidence of our neglect is available in an analysis of our current growth in employment. Between 1973 and 1979, we added about thirteen million new nonagricultural jobs to the American economy, a remarkable achievement that far outstrips any of our competitors. Many take comfort in that fact as the final proof of the health of the American economic system. I do not. What disturbs me is that the growth was concentrated in low-wage and low-productivity jobs, which offer short hours and low wages. They tend to be dead-end jobs. What is most disturbing is that they tend to concentrate among women and new entrants to the labor market upon whom our future productivity depends. In sum, a significant portion of the growth in the American economy is leading toward an economic structure characterized by badly paid and unproductive work.

The most disturbing evidence comes from a series of studies suggesting that our failing competitive advantage in foreign markets is due, in part, to our underinvestment in human capital. Most recently, the Bureau of International Labor Affairs reports that the decline in U.S. trade performance since the 1960s results from differences both in the growth of net real investment in equipment *and* in the development of labor skills acquired through education and training. Between 1963 and 1975, the U.S. share of the world's skilled workers fell from 29 percent to 26 percent. Internationally, we dropped from second to seventh in the "skill endowments" of our workers. The result of these ominous trends is that the skill content of American imports increases while American exports steadily lose their competitive advantage.

We continue to ignore the importance of human capital in the overall performance of the economy at our peril. We have arrived at a perplexing point where we experience both high unemployment and skill shortages. What's more, shortages are likely to become more severe. Massive new public commitments to surges in defense and energy production will likely result in further shortages and consequent inflationary bottlenecks in production. Our military buildup guarantees that, in addition to policies to

ensure an available skilled work force for military production, we
will need to carefully cater to the needs of civilian industries lest
they become starved for skilled workers and capital.

Competition for high technology production will increase among
industrialized nations. That competition accelerates even now.
Technological shifts can come with dizzying speed. Their implication for current modes of production and labor force requirements can be profound. For instance, if technological changes in
the Rolls Royce had proceeded at the same rate as changes in the
electronics industry since the early 1970s, a Rolls Royce would
be one and one-half feet in length, would travel up to speeds of
ten million miles per hour, and would cost no more that $2.75.

A rapidly shifting industrial base and accelerating international
competition will increase the need for occupational and geographic
mobility in the nation's labor force. Both will be more difficult
as the labor force ages. Nothing threatens growth more than the
proliferation of defensive "protectionist" measures to protect workers from structural changes. In order to avoid protectionism, we
need a long-term commitment to continuous skill upgrading, education, and training for all workers.

What's more, as we become a more labor-intensive service
economy, productivity improvements will increasingly be embodied in human rather than machine capital. In 1978, the share of
the service sector in employment reached 68 percent and accounted for 66 percent of the GNP. According to the latest projection, that sector will grow faster than any other between now
and 1990.

Finally, the age profile of the American work force will demand
greater output per worker. Before World War II, the ratio of
workers to nonworkers was 9 to 1. In 1981, the ratio dropped to
3 to 1. In 1990, the ratio will be 2 to 1. Marked increases in
worker productivity will be required to support the after-tax earnings on workers at reasonable levels and to maintain a growing
dependent population.

From Baby Boom to Baby Bust

Demography will be the most telling factor for the future of training. Labor force growth will decline from the current 2.2 percent
per annum to as little as nine-tenths of 1 percent per annum in

1990. Human capital should become more valuable to public, private, and military institutions as it becomes more scarce. Optimistic but defensible projections suggest that unemployment could fall to 4.5 percent by 1990, even assuming moderate economic growth. A higher growth scenario could drop the rate as low as 4 percent. Moreover, some analysts suggest that current wage minimums, Social Security taxes, and a series of other disincentives add as much as 1.5 percent to the current unemployment rate. Inflation and statutory changes may eliminate a significant proportion of this kind of unemployment by the early 1990s, allowing for an unemployment rate below 4 per cent.

If these trends hold, therefore, employment will not be the problem in the late 1980s and early 1990s. The political issue to come will be wages, not jobs. The wage problem will be especially severe if current trends are allowed to continue. Assuming our underinvestment in human capital persists, a significant share of our work force will be employed, but stuck in low-wage, low-productivity jobs. The only way we will be able to beat the wage problem is with productivity increases that justify sufficient wages to maintain workers and nonworkers. A broadly based machine and human capital investment strategy would seem a logical response to the productivity problem.

The need for accelerated investment in human capital will become even more urgent in the future as most of our labor force growth will come from women and minorities, where our current deficits in human capital are greatest. Under any set of economic assumptions, women will make up fully two thirds of the labor force growth between now and 1990. While the proportion of other population groups will decline, minorities will comprise an increased share of the population and the labor force. These populations are likely to find work, but in low-wage/low-productivity service jobs in the private sector. We will no longer be faced so much with the problem of finding private sector work for women and minorities as much as increasing their productivity sufficiently to justify higher wages. In my view, that is a happy problem. In the absence of a human capital strategy, I'm afraid it will become what the great philosopher Pogo calls an "insurmountable opportunity."

Flies in the Ointment: Technology and Economic Policy

There are, as always, flies in the ointment. One fly is technology. Analysts of the employment impact of technology fall into two camps: the optimists and the pessimists. The pessimists point out that technology, especially microelectronics, is about to come through on the automation threats of twenty years ago. In addition, if one matches economic sectors where the projected employment growth is highest between now and 1990, with likely technological advances in the workplace, one discovers that those sectors currently projected to generate the most new jobs stand directly in the new technology's line of march.

The optimists point out that historical experience and their own projection suggest that when all is said and done, the application of new technologies creates new productivity, products, and wealth, which in turn creates demand for new products and services, thereby creating more, not fewer jobs. Optimists recognize that those who are technologically displaced are, of course, not the same people who will qualify for new jobs created by general economic expansion. Optimists resolve this difficulty with the "mix" of labor skills by calling for constant retraining.

I think the optimists have the better of the argument, but only if we can agree with them that the American economy can transform new technology into low-cost marketable goods. If we cannot complete the cycle from new technology to higher quality and reduced prices, we will not make the gains in international competitive advantage sufficient to expand market shares and provide additional jobs for the United States.

Therein lies the second fly in the ointment. Our ability to translate new technology into lower prices, higher quality, and increased market shares is largely dependent on the general economic environment and the policies and practices that create it. The avoidance of restrictive practices, ranging from labor protections that discourage reduced costs to the tendency for managers to invest in ongoing concerns on financial paper rather than production, will largely determine our success. Moreover, restrictive national economic policies that encourage high interest rates and unemployment will further impede the overall demand conditions necessary to the transition of technological gain in productivity and wealth and into new production and jobs.

Guidelines for Strategic Thinking

With those cautions aside, let me turn briefly to a broad set of guidelines for a human capital strategy for the future. First, we should learn to educate and train much more flexibly in both educational and business institutions. In educational institutions we need more job-specific training, and in private firms we need to provide education beyond that required for simple tasks. As a nation we have not overinvested in general education; we have underinvested in job-related preparation. To use one aggregate but telling statistic: Since 1960 we have produced about 85 percent more college grads and only 1.4 percent more white-collar jobs. If we are going to produce a broadly educated population we must arm them with skills that enable them to make a living.

Demography pretty well guarantees that education and training will have to be more job-related; with the "baby bust" and receding incentives for early retirement, the labor force will age. The training client will more and more often be an adult with prior work history, ready for job-specific training or retraining with a minimum of remediation. As a result, job-specific training, currently the province of a $40 billion private training enterprise, will likely become an increasing proportion of a worker's total education.

Let me add that it is not necessarily true that private training will automatically expand fully with a greater commitment to it. Businesses will exercise their option to "make or buy" additional training. Providers of various kinds, including post-secondary institutions, will benefit from the decision to "buy."

Second, the trend toward reduced isolation of post-secondary systems should be encouraged. Our historical labor surplus has encouraged the extension of adolescence and the sequestering of the young apart from the matrix of social relations in which they must eventually interact. The alienation of the young has implications far beyond the nation's problems of economic efficiency.

To those who argue that universities should not be bastardized in the interest of industrial requirements, I offer the view that no one would sensibly propose anything of the kind. To the contrary, I believe that more community involvement would improve the fundamental quality of academic disciplines, especially the social sciences. Political science is dead, because it eschews the study of bureaucracy, the most important political phenomenon since the industrial revolution, in favor of the pretentiously quantitative study of voting behavior. Public administration, which does concern itself with the intellectual dilemma of bureaucracy, survives as a moneymaker in many universities, but as a second-class citizen in the intellectual pecking order of academe. American economics began on the right track with the institutionalist perspectives of the pre-Keynesian "Texas school," but has long since surrendered relevance to the ontology of "economic man," the epistemology of a native positivism, and the methodology of recondite econometric modeling. In short, in a time of rapid change the abandonment of isolation will enable institutions of higher learning to better explain the world to all of us who must live in it. Our adaptability will depend on the generic understanding it provides. This will be all the more important as students increasingly come from nontraditional groups, especially older workers updating job skills.

Third, education and training improvements can and should be largely paid for by the private firms and individuals that benefit from them. The first priority for available public funds must be to provide the full range of remediation services for those most in need. Since much of the benefit from job-specific training accrues to individual and private firms, it is entirely conceivable and appropriate that these beneficiaries pay most of the cost.

Fourth, if there are to be public subsidies, they should be for voluntary and nonbureaucratic devices such as loans, tax incentives, and vouchers that provide incentives, but leave the initiative to participate with firms or individuals.

Fifth, a reformation of education and training policies toward more privately based job-specific strategies will require a highly decentralized delivery system. No nationwide policy can account for the geographic and industrial diversity in the American economy. A subnational focus for education and training policy is best served by delivery systems that allow for education and training decision-making at the initiative of private individuals and firms. We need to recognize that the national economy is a statistical creation. The government's encouragement of nationwide economic policies unfortunately tends to ignore the flesh and bone of subnational economic development. The economy builds from the bottom up and not from the top down.

Mechanisms

It is standard practice in the recent American experience to respond to some perceived need with a full array of programs, personnel, and promotion. In my view nothing grand is advisable at this point. I do not intend to deny the need. My remarks to this point demonstrate my own concern. Where mechanisms are concerned, however, I am an incrementalist at heart. In my view the breadth of the task, to craft a strategy for improving the quality of the entire labor force, demands an incrementalist approach.

There are other reasons to go slowly. First, the American social structure separates public and private in a very complex fashion. Our system pursues the public interest through a melange of mechanisms that mix public incentives and private initiatives. Any attempt to build full-blown mechanisms for a labor market strategy is likely to disrupt the seamless web of current public and private relations and ultimately fail. Second, we are as yet unsure of the nature and extent of the problem we intend to address. We are at the edge of economic changes that are unprecedented, if not in kind, then certainly in the accelerated rate at which they are occurring. We need to understand those economic processes better before we can assess their implications for fruitful human resource strategies. Third and finally, awareness of the importance of an adaptable and quality work force for the future overall performance of the American economy is not broadcast. That awareness needs to be built on the solid foundation of practical understanding. We are ill-advised to grab hold of the most recent shortage statistics and run off like Henny Penny to announce yet another "crisis." In fact, I think the "crisis" will never come. Instead, we will continue the steady numbing progression of productivity decline and protectionist barriers to economic growth.

Revitalization Centers

Before we launch any leaky new boats we should consider resources already available that can be mobilized by effective leadership. I propose we follow the path of least resistance, and in that spirit I offer the notion of industry-based "revitalization centers." Such centers would rely on private initiative and public tax expenditure. In my judgment no new tax expenditures or any other laws need be enacted to create these centers. They would be funded through the recently expanded research and development tax write-offs. The centers could be created at the plant, firm, or industry level and would be governed as private authorities saw fit. The centers could be involved in a range of activities. Those created at the industry level could, for instance, provide both national and international trend information on trade, financial markets, labor markets, etc. In a sense, privately based industry-level institutions could perform industry policy functions normally shared by government and labor authorities in other nations. As a result, it might be possible to build an industrial policy capability into the American system without doing violence to traditional public/private relations.

At the firm and plant level, revitalization centers could assume a whole series of planning, R&D application, process research, training, and retraining functions already underway in varying degrees among bellwether plants and firms. Where small businesses, individual firms, and plants do not realize economies of scale sufficient to encourage their participation, firm and plant consortia could be allowed. In addition, where R&D credits do not apply, centers could be supported through the pooling of tax losses and an expanded gift tax credit.

The benefit to higher education is apparent, I hope. Let me spell it out just to be sure. An expansion in privately based revitalization efforts will necessarily draw on higher education resources. The centers would also supply an institutional vehicle for cooperative utilization of resources, obviating the current "raiding."

Expanding Education and Training

There are a variety of current proposals for expanding the nation's human capital investment. With the exception of those that suggest direct subsidies to firms, most would allow subsidy for both firm-based and post-secondary education and training. As you know, even firm-based subsidies can result in expanded post-secondary activities, according to whether firms decide to "make" or "buy" education and training.

The most often suggested mechanisms for expanding education and training are tax subsidies and vouchers. For example, business firms might be given tax credits for part of an increase in training expenditures over the average amount spent during the previous three years. With a 10 percent tax credit, every $1 billion of additional private sector training generated by the credit would result in direct costs to the U.S. Treasury of only $100 million lost in tax revenues. The returns from increased productivity, reduced inflation, reduced public dependency, and higher taxable income and profits would be significant in the short term and would represent an inestimable net gain over the long haul.

Vouchers and credits, on the other hand, can be designed to leave control of education and training decisions with workers rather than employers. For instance, displaced workers could be given a training subsidy to be cashed in by a business firm or a post-secondary institution, allowing the worker to shop around. Another way would be to expand individual income tax deductions that are currently limited to education and training related to a person's existing job. Deductions or tax credits might be allowed for educational training costs leading to new jobs in growth or skill shortage industries.

Both tax subsidies and vouchers are conceptually appealing, because even ambitious goals can be pursued with a minimum of public bureaucracy. But both have significant design problems:

- Unless public subsidies are carefully structured, they may pay for private sector training that would have occurred anyway.
- Subsidies limited to net new training investments might require bookkeeping and enforcement provisions that would discourage business use.
- Overly aggressive targeting of subsidies on high-risk individuals will unnecessarily brand recipients as undesirable employees and reduce business participation—especially by growth firms with less need for public subsidies.
- Public subsidies may be wasted on large firms, which realize sufficient returns from self-financed training efforts so that they may not be influenced by public subsidies.

In structuring tax or voucher mechanisms, the design problems will need careful attention. In particular, efforts to target subsidies must achieve a careful balance between social goals and the realities of private production. Since private firms operate for profit and not for social gain, they will hire and train the cream among available applicants. Although "creaming" has become a pejorative term in public debate, it is clear that incentives for upgrading existing workers, or for hiring and training those first in line, will shorten the queue of unemployed workers and create vacancies in entry-level jobs.

The experience of other nations with universal training subsidies suggests another potential model for expanding human capital investment in the United States. Workers as well as employers would contribute toward financing a training fund through payroll taxes, and be able to draw on the fund up to a certain amount throughout their lifetimes to pay for job-specific training. Special "set-asides" also could be provided to extend similar benefits to new entrants to the labor force or to the long-term unemployed.

The major problem with this approach is its cost; funding through already overworked payroll taxes would be unthinkable in the near future. Design problems include the potential for the universal entitlement nature of the subsidy to encourage casual and inefficient usage by workers and the inequities for those who are taxed but never use the entitlement.

Creating loan funds for use by individuals, businesses, or other institutions in obtaining or providing job-specific training has the advantage of imposing training costs on participants through loan repayment. Loans would be attractive to private institutions and individuals by reducing the strain on cash flow that private financing of training creates. This would also accomplish the goal of putting human capital investments on the same long-term financial footing as machine capital. Public costs would arise from capitalizing these loan funds initially, covering loan defaults, and perhaps subsidizing loan terms for disadvantaged clients. But an expanded federal funding role could be avoided if current federally financed general education loans were altered to focus on job-specific training.

Among existing programs, cooperative education—simultaneous schooling and work experience—provides a ready and expandable model for reducing the isolation of schooling from the world of work. That isolation may have been convenient when labor was oversupplied, but makes less sense as the labor force shrinks. Despite the relative success and popularity of coop-ed programs, federal encouragement of this approach has actually lessened in recent years. The tools for expanding this model are readily available in federal funding for secondary, post-secondary, and vocational education.

All the mechanisms addressed so far would increase the numbers of people seeking training without necessarily expanding the quantity or quality of the nation's plant, equipment, and personnel for supplying training. Among the options for creating training infrastructure are:

- Tax credits to help cover business costs for training equipment, teaching facilities, instructors, and teaching technology.
- Encouraging cooperative use of public and private education and training resources through changes in the current gift tax, or other provisions supporting the transfer and full use of instructors, space, and equipment among public and private institutions.
- Allowing individual firms or consortia to use tax write-offs for training research and development that are now available for other private sector R&D purposes.
- Providing training infrastructure loans, as in the case where a group of small firms seeks to create a consortium training entity to handle training needs that cannot be met by individual firms.

To be fully effective, many of the options described above would require a network of public/private "brokering" entities—perhaps voluntary labor/management/government boards operating at the labor market or other levels—perhaps the Revitalization Center discussed earlier. Many large firms, for example, while not easily influenced by automatic public subsidies, would be amenable to sharing the use of their own training facilities to achieve broader public goals as long as basic add-on costs were covered and arrangements avoided bureaucratic intervention. Privately controlled agents are needed to play brokering or "deal-making" roles in these and other situations, such as the formulation of small firm training consortia and facilitating business understanding and use of tax and other public training incentives.

In fact, one short-term alternative to the dramatic departure from current federal policy sketched in this article is a more cautious effort to build complementary public/private training strategies through support of voluntary labor/management/government boards. These boards could take on a variety of advisory and other functions as they evolved. However, they would need

to avoid becoming cumbersome administrative agencies themselves instead of supplanting existing public bureaucracies.

The mechanisms cited above provide only a brief glimpse of
the types of options available to decision-makers in developing
a human capital policy for the future. The key issue is the need
for nontraditional approaches to meet the changing and growing
labor force problems that will inevitably require a response if the
United States is to achieve continued economic growth.

Chapter 7

TAX POLICY: SOME ISSUES FOR HIGHER EDUCATION

by JoAnn Moody

This chapter briefly focuses on several exemptions from taxation which benefit higher education in New England and elsewhere and several other exemptions or tax changes that would bring further aid.

Higher education is one of New England's largest industries.[1] The region boasts a diversity and wealth of private and public campuses. Moreover, the research universities of the region have been instrumental in helping to transform New England's economy from labor-intensive with concentrations in manufacturing to knowledge-intensive with concentrations in technology-based services and products. There is every indication that these centers of advanced knowledge will take a more central role in bolstering the economy of this region.[2]

The first section of this chapter focuses on taxes and the institutions. Specifically, I examine the sometimes controversial exemption from local property tax granted to campuses. I also examine the business income tax exemption (state and federal) granted to campuses for their research-related endeavors. The new federal patent law affecting universities and small businesses is discussed because it will undoubtedly enable universities to increase the "passive" non-taxable income which they can realize through commercial development of discoveries made during federally funded research on their campuses. Finally, I suggest a few ways in which the New England states can enhance the growing importance of their universities to the region's economy.

The second section, entitled "Taxes and the Donors," highlights

125

the new cuts in federal tax rates for individuals and corporations which, ironically, will mean a lower level of charitable donations for campuses. In this sense the Economic Recovery Tax Act of 1981 is not a blessing for higher education. Several incentives are set out which at the state level might increase the private support for higher education, especially for research and technical education.

The final section, entitled "Taxes, Parents, and Students," briefly touches on several tax breaks often proposed for parents and one for students. The aid to students would allow graduates to characterize some of the higher education costs they incurred as a "necessary" business expense—one which could then be deducted over time from their federal or state gross income.

While this chapter is not exhaustive, it is meant to highlight for both citizens and policy-makers several important issues now facing higher education.

Taxes and the Institutions

In recognition of the important service of providing higher education to citizens, states grant exemptions from taxation to eligible private, not-for-profit higher education institutions. States typically accept the eligibility determination made by the U.S. Internal Revenue Service pursuant to its Code Section 501(c)(3) describing not-for-profit corporations operated exclusively for educational purposes. Those educational institutions granted exemption status may operate without the encumbrance of the business income tax, property tax, sales tax, capital gains tax, and property transfer tax.[3]

Tax-exempt status is also invaluable because institutions possessing it may receive charitable contributions from individuals and corporations which are tax deductible, within limits, to the donor.[4] Moreover, a donor's gift through his or her will to an exempt campus can be used as a deduction, with no ceiling, to reduce the estate taxes due.[5] These tax breaks to institutions plus tax incentives to donors constitute an important part of support to higher education.[6] Because they are entities of the state, public campuses enjoy the same exemptions and benefit from the same encouragement to charitable donors as private campuses.

The Property Tax Exemption

Tax-exempt status relieves a campus, public or private, of property tax set by the town or city or county where the campus is located. Thus dormitories, academic buildings, and campus grounds are typically tax-free. But this exemption sometimes provokes the ire of officials and citizens of a county or municipality who struggle to pay for local police, fire, school, health, and other services from the tax assessments of real property within their jurisdictions. Resentment by some communities seems to be a cyclical[7] occurrence.

The City of Boston provides several instructive examples which have and undoubtedly will again be repeated in various parts of New England. Arguing that the City cannot pay for public services out of its present tax revenues and that passage of Proposition 2½ (the so-called "property taxpayers' revolt")[8] has exacerbated the problem, Boston in its 1981 Fiscal Legislative Proposals to the state legislature asked unsuccessfully for several changes.[9] The City asked the legislature to repeal the tax-exempt status of housing owned by higher education institutions (public and private). Moreover, it proposed that the state be required to make payments to localities in lieu of tax payments on behalf of both public and private institutions. Thirdly, the City proposed that the legislature grant localities the authority to impose a local-option excise tax on students. This so-called "student head tax" could be fixed at not more than $75 for one full-time student (public and private) and would be justified, according to the City, because students presently receive local services but do not contribute to meet the cost of those services. Several months later, in December 1981, Boston City Hall presented and then withdrew a proposal to impose a firefighters user fee on public and private colleges, universities, and commercial establishments which require more than average fire protection.[10]

These examples of discontent by one locality are not unique. Responding to direct and indirect complaints, several private colleges and universities throughout New England have voluntarily made annual contributions, albeit small, to help pay the local costs of fire, police, and other community services. Other colleges, on the other hand, remain adamantly opposed to such contributions and argue that they already carry their own weight in that they perform a significant public service for both the community and

the state and generate considerable revenue into the local and
state economy.

Solutions to the Property Tax Problem

Change in Public Opinion. Because the property-tax problem
may be exaggerated and misunderstood, it is crucial to improve
the public's understanding. For example, the real culprit may be
government. This conclusion is reached when one compares the
land area and assessed value of the property occupied by tax-
exempt municipal, state, and federal governments, public gardens
and parks, and so on with that of exempt private colleges and
universities.[11] For instance, in Boston for fiscal year 1979, 78
percent of the exempt land area (13,410 acres) was occupied by
federal, state, and city buildings and facilities. Such government
occupation accounted for 38 percent of the total land area of the
city. On the other hand, private colleges and universities occupied
only 2.8 percent of the total land area and only 5.7 percent of
exempt land area.[12]

Therefore it is naive, according to the Massachusetts Taxpayers
Foundation, to blame private colleges and universities for Boston's
fiscal problems.[13] It should be acknowledged, nonetheless, that
Boston as a state capital would possess an unusually large number
of government buildings.

According to Table 7–1, the assessed valuation of tax-exempt
property belonging to cities and towns in Massachusetts totaled
$4,767,840,762 for fiscal year 1979. The assessed valuation of tax-
exempt property belonging to the state totaled $2,069,385,721.
That of private colleges and universities totaled $1,638,050,683.
This table also sets out the assessed value of property held by
charities, churches, cemeteries, and other eligible societies.

What must be remembered is that localities throughout the
region and country determine assessed valuation of exempt property in different ways. The figures provided here for valuation of
exempt property do not reflect the fair market value of that property. The different valuation systems also tend to invalidate reliable comparisons between one locality and another.[14]

Nonetheless, it is safe to say that private colleges account for
only a small fraction of the total tax-exempt land area and valuation
in a state. By far the largest exempt holdings are those of local,
state, and federal governments. Even though of all the New En-

Table 7–1   Tax-Exempt Real Estate Valuation by Categories

Categories	Valuation, FY 1979	
	Boston	Massachusetts
United States of America	$100,682,500	$ 518,216,966
Housing authorities	123,895,700	746,498,111
Commonwealth of Massachusetts	665,384,600	2,069,385,721
Literary (including Independent Colleges and Universities)	256,170,800	1,638,050,683
Benevolent	209,640,100	482,150,045
Charitable	92,437,500	683,389,540
Scientific institutions	9,319,400	92,284,270
Temperance societies	186,400	579,000
Agriculture societies	850,000	10,073,721
War veterans organizations	798,700	21,320,648
Military organizations	40,000	40,000
Parsonages	540,414	62,790,061
Churches	12,353,244	617,414,922
Cemeteries	6,511,400	51,643,953
Water companies	—	250,270
Municipal (cities and towns)	569,601,900	4,767,840,762
Counties	2,838,000	140,770,507
Public districts	—	421,325,417

SOURCE: Massachusetts Department of Revenue, fiscal year 1979. Table organized by James A. True, Association of Independent Colleges and Universities in Massachusetts.

gland states Massachusetts has the largest number of private colleges and universities, the valuation of exempt property belonging to these institutions equals less than one fourth of the valuation of government property in the state.[15] If the public at large and especially local officials and citizens understood this, they might feel less resentful.

There are several reasons why the public should view property tax exemption for colleges and universities as a wise economic *investment* for taxpayers and, indeed, as a cost-saver rather than a drain. For example, if private colleges were forced to pay property taxes, the operating budgets of some would rise as much as 40 percent.[16] That added cost would necessarily be passed on to students, with only wealthy students escaping hardship while low- and middle-income students and their families would acutely feel the pressure. Moreover, the added cost of property taxes would force some private colleges to close down, thereby sending more students into state-funded public institutions. This shift would not mean a savings for the taxpayer because the public taxes needed to educate the extra students would far exceed the value of the exemption previously granted to the now defunct private colleges.

Closing down a private college would also harm the economy of the locality where the college is located. Numerous college employees and suppliers would be out of work. The locality's tax base would correspondingly suffer from the loss of money once generated into the economy by the college and the loss of tax money paid by college employees. Loss of some private institutions would also destroy the variety of educational settings and offerings now available to residents. The students' "freedom of educational choice" would be compromised.

In an important sense, private colleges "earn" the exemption they are granted. Their students, faculty, and staff donate their volunteer services in various ways to boards, agencies, and community groups in the localities and states. Colleges often provide their own campus police, sidewalk maintenance, and similar otherwise public services in order to minimize their burden on the host community. Private colleges distribute financial aid to needy residents through private scholarships. And the colleges appreciably enrich the cultural and recreational life of the community by inviting the public to campus activities, allowing public use of recreational facilities and meeting rooms, and by increasingly providing continuing education programs for elders and other adults in the community. It is argued that these specific benefits, as well as providing the general good of education to the public, justify the exemption from local property tax granted to private campuses.[17]

Public institutions can legitimately use some of these same arguments. The faculty, students, and staff of public colleges and universities often donate their expertise and time to community activities. Requiring the public campuses to pay property tax would in effect be allowing the local government to tax the state government. (Yet it can be argued that fairness requires taxpayers from across the state to contribute to paying the local tax bill of the state school—rather than leaving the burden solely on citizens who happen to have the state institution within their locality's borders.) State campuses enhance a community's economy as well as its cultural and recreational life. If a locality were permitted to tax the property of a public campus, the students would be forced to pay considerably higher tuition. Only wealthy students would escape the hardship.[18]

In summary, the public may be insufficiently informed of how colleges and universities do "carry" their own weight and generate income into a locality's economy. Moreover, the public may not realize that government buildings and grounds rather than colleges and universities typically make up the greatest part of a state's tax-exempt property. With sufficient information, local officials and citizens might feel less resentment toward public and private educational institutions located in their community.

On the other hand, public understanding may not be enough. Several states in New England have taken steps to help localities recapture some of the revenue lost from tax-exempt schools.

State Reimbursement to Localities. Three states in New England have procedures in place for reimbursing localities for part of the tax revenue lost because higher education campuses are located within their bounds. Connecticut in 1978 enacted a reimbursement system which pays back to the locality 25 percent of the annual tax revenue lost from real property (land and improvements) that is owned by a private, nonprofit, and tax-exempt institution of higher education. The locality's tax rate is used in determining the reimbursement due. Efforts to pass a reimbursement plan for public campuses have thus far been unsuccessful.[19]

Maine recently enacted a statute covering private institutions which orders the state treasurer to reimburse each municipality 50 percent of the property tax exemptions granted after April 1, 1978. This means that any new category of exemptions created by the legislature after this date will be covered by the statute. Thus far no new categories have been granted.[20]

While several attempts to pass a Connecticut-like reimbursement plan have been made in Massachusetts, thus far none has been successful. Massachusetts at present provides for reimbursement to each locality only for tax revenues lost on land (not buildings) that is occupied by public institutions such as the University of Massachusetts, the University of Lowell, and Southeastern Massachusetts University—but not community colleges. While the formula calls for a return to the locality of the tax revenues lost on the market value of the land, the legislature can underfund the reimbursement. The formula also uses the average state tax rate, not the locality's average rate.[21]

Clearly, state reimbursement of at least part of lost revenues is an attractive solution. Some argue that it is more equitable for localities with institutions, whether public or private, to bear only part of the tax burden and to receive supplemental payments from taxpayers throughout the state. On the other hand, those same localities are enjoying economic and cultural benefits not shared by localities which have no campus within their boundaries.

Research and Development by Universities

Universities are increasingly involved in raising tax-free revenues, not only through research contracts with private industry but also by commercial exploitation of discoveries made by their faculty. Although small colleges will probably be unable to compete in these research circles and thereby generate revenue, research universities are now exploring ways to benefit from the revolutionary advances in such fields as biogenetics, agriculture and horticulture, computer technology, robotics, and microelectronics being made in their campus laboratories.

New England universities have been rightfully credited with bolstering, in an indispensable manner, the new knowledge-intensive economy of the region. During the past three decades this economy has dramatically shifted from a labor-intensive system with concentration in manufacturing of textiles, shoes, and other durables to a knowledge-intensive economy with concentration in technology-related businesses and services in computers, health care, electronics, and precision instrumentation. Universities have been the key to the creation of this sophisticated, technological economy through spin-off industries started by highly skilled faculty and graduates.

But universities are now involved with more than indirect spin-offs. They are directly creating new enterprises and product lines as they increasingly hold patents and grant licenses to businesses to commercially develop their discoveries. They are sometimes choosing to invest in these development firms and, in a few cases, to wholly own the firms.

Revenues from Research Contracts

Universities are now relying more and more on private industry to fund campus research projects. Due to the cutbacks in federal money for these projects, university partnerships with the private sector have taken on new importance.[22]

Research contracts are exempted from the federal business income tax by the Internal Revenue Code. Code sections exclude from taxation all income which an educational institution derives from research for a federal or state agency as well as for any private person or company.[23] In the case of a university's nonprofit research institute (such as the Wisconsin Alumni Research Foundation formed in 1925 and the Purdue Foundation in 1930[24]), the income derived from a research contract with any person or company is tax exempt if the results are freely available to the public.

The shift from federal funding to business funding is exemplified by the research budget of Carnegie-Mellon University in Pittsburgh. During fiscal year 1981, one third of the campus's $36.3 million research budget came from industry. Ten percent is the present figure for other universities,[25] although in 1978 only 3.7 percent of research expenditures flowed from industry.[26] The ratio at Carnegie-Mellon is rising rapidly as the university builds on its strengths in robotics, microelectronics, computer technology, and combustion engineering. Ten million more private dollars per year are expected for the robotics program alone.[27]

Business funding of university research should also expand because of a change in the federal tax law. President Reagan's Economic Recovery Act of 1981 grants a tax credit to business of 65 percent of amounts paid to a research firm or university for contract research and 65 percent of corporate grants for basic research to be performed by universities and research institutes. The effective period of this tax credit is after June 30, 1981 and before January 1, 1986.[28] In effect, the federal government is making a "matching" contribution to the university (in the form of lost taxes) each time a business claims a tax credit for research expenditures.[29]

Revenues from University-Held Patents and Copyrights

In 1974 a comprehensive study of revenues made by university patent programs showed that $100,000 was the average net annual royalty income made by the three universities with the most active programs.[30] Today there are much higher hopes that substantial revenue can be generated by university exploitation of patents and copyrights. "Across the country" patent and copyright licensing staffs are being assembled or expanded in the universities and in their research institutes.[31]

At Stanford in 1981 $700,000 in royalty income was earned from a patent in music engineering. A music professor developed a software chip for the design of music synthesizers to which Yamaha of Japan purchased a license. This software development was copyrighted, as will probably be the sophisticated software developed in much of genetic technology. In 1981, $1.2 million was earned by Stanford's copyrights and patents. According to Stanford regulations, one third of the royalties go to the inventor, one third to the department, and one third to the school.[32]

The income from patents, licenses, and copyrights received by a university is regarded by the federal tax code as "passive" income excludable from taxation, just as are rents and interest payments received. Royalties are not considered to be business income generated by unrelated business activities, which is taxable.[33]

Besides these generous tax rules, educational institutions will benefit from a new patent law which was signed by President Carter and became effective July 1, 1981. The new patent law (Title 35, Chapter 18, Sections 200–211 of the *U.S. Code Annotated*) in most cases places title to a discovery made during a federal research project in the hands of the university or small business conducting the research. Moreover, the new patent law encourages new profit-making partnerships between small business and higher education campuses and protects the ownership of an invention even as it provides for rapid and practical development and application of that invention. In general, the new law strives to make America more competitive with other advanced countries, Japan especially, in the fields of technological innovation and development.

The patent changes are enormously significant because they presume that, from the beginning, title to an invention discovered during a federally funded project resides with the college or small business firm and not the federal government. Secondly, the changes cut down on red tape and administrative headaches by consolidating more than 20 different government rules covering the patenting and licensing of inventions. The law also speeds up the entire process of patenting and licensing and thus hastens prompt and full public use of the invention. General Counsel and Director of the Patent, Copyright and Licensing Offices of the Massachusetts Institute of Technology, Arthur A. Smith, has hailed the simplifying effects of the new law.[34]

One particular objective of the Patent Act is set forth in its Section 200: "To promote collaboration between commercial concerns and nonprofit organizations, including universities." Section

202(c)(7) (see Appendix) shows how that collaboration could work. A nonprofit organization could assign (that is, sell or transfer) the rights of its invention to an invention-management firm but not to a manufacturing company or retailer.

Second, the educational institution could grant an exclusive license to use and market the patented invention to a small business firm for the 17-year life of the patent—but to a licensee other than a small business for no more than 5 years. Third, the institution would be required to share an unspecified amount of the earned royalties with the inventor. Finally, and probably most importantly, the net income from any royalties must be used by the institution for the support of "scientific research or education," as opposed presumably to general educational purposes.

Section 204, entitled "Preference for U.S. Industry," forbids both a nonprofit organization and a small business firm from licensing the right to use or sell the invention to a person or company in the United States unless the products to be manufactured will be made "substantially" in this country. Nonetheless, the Act does not prohibit the holder of a patented invention from granting a license to a foreign corporation which will sell or manufacture outside the United States.[35]

Finally, small businesses and educational institutions and other nonprofit organizations are afforded greater "business secret" protection by the new law. Section 205, entitled "Confidentiality," authorizes federal agencies to withhold from public disclosure critical information about the new discovery while the business or organization formally applies for a patent.

Thus this new law is designed to bring about new partnerships between businesses and educational institutions in the commercial development of inventions. If the college or university chooses not to spend its net income from invention royalties on further scientific research and education, then it is unclear what the federal government could or would do. One argument by a university could be that the government relinquished all power over the invention (even though it funded the research project) and thus has no authority to supervise how the royalties are spent.

New Models for University Involvement

As universities continue to explore money-making ventures in high technology, controversy will inevitably swirl. For some higher education leaders it is the best of times, for others the worst of times.

Harvard's president, Derek Bok, has warned of the enormous conflicts of interest which will confront faculty and administrators who try to straddle the commercial and academic worlds. He has advised against Harvard's becoming an original and substantial investor in a biotechnology firm, Biogen, started by a Harvard biologist, because conflicts could arise in determining faculty promotion, leaves of absence, and lab space for faculty engaged in such a company. Bok further warns that some faculty may come to regard their research findings as business secrets to be protected rather than as contributions to a universal body of public knowledge, traditionally to be shared, and that professors doubling as entrepreneurs may be diverted from their normal academic responsibilities, to the detriment of students and the university. For the same reasons, President Bok advised against Harvard starting up an independent foundation to commercialize new discoveries made by Harvard faculty.[36]

On the other hand, MIT as well as Stanford University and Berkeley, among others, have eagerly sanctioned close partnership of the commercial and academic spheres. The two California campuses, for example, have formed an agreement with a bioengineering company, Engenics. The company has issued 30 percent of its equity to a nonprofit center, to be held in trust for the support of future research at the two universities. Moreover, the center has started off with $10 million contributed by six major corporations. The companies will simultaneously be funding basic university research through the center and the commercial application of that research through Engenics.

In this instance the universities have avoided the Harvard problem because they are not shareholders in a company created by faculty members. Yet the universities will receive, for research purposes, a major share of capital gains and dividends generated by Engenics. "It's a new model, both for obtaining corporate support for university research, and for technology transfer from the laboratory to the marketable product," according to Stanford's president, Donald Kennedy.[37]

Another model is being tested at Tufts University Medical School in Boston. Members of the molecular biology and microbiology department have recently formed a research partnership, separate from the university but consisting solely of faculty mem-

bers from that department. The partnership—called "Micromole"—
is designed to avoid conflicts of interest by selecting outside consulting projects that do not closely overlap research underway in
their Tufts laboratories. The partnership is also designed to be
an open and cohesive unit, which will avoid the bad feelings often
produced when faculty of a department go off in different directions.[38]

Finally, in the fall of 1981 MIT's faculty overwhelmingly approved the formation at MIT of a $125 million Whitehead Institute
for research in developmental biology, specifically concerning
processes of cell fertilization, division, and differentiation. The
director and the thirteen researchers will have joint Whitehead–MIT
appointments. Patents will be owned by the institute, with royalties shared with MIT after deductions for a variety of operating
expenses. In effect, MIT has surrendered control of patent policy
to the Whitehead Institute, which will decide to whom the patent
licenses will be sold. This shift in control is upsetting to some
faculty but will insulate MIT from product liability suits should
a product line go awry. Also upsetting to some faculty is the
conflict of interest that will inevitably face the researchers who
hold joint appointments and thus "serve two masters."[39]

Most faculty, however, believe the risk is worth taking, that
the benefit to MIT is exciting, and that sensible rules will evolve.
Moreover, several insist that the entrepreneurial spirit needs to
be fostered at MIT and other educational institutions in order to
meet the challenges brought by Japan and West Germany.[40]

While controversy will continue over the university's place in
commercial development, the current flux created in the scientific
community is healthy, according to arguments by some faculty.
America will be strengthened by the "movement of people back
and forth between companies and universities. It stimulates the
general level of science where it is permitted, and in many places
science is static because there's no moving around."[41] Others argue
that faculty members' consulting with the government and the
private sector has always been complex and that this "underground
economy" resulting from the straddling of the academic and outside worlds is nothing new.[42]

While that may be true, the university itself is playing a more
central role in its effort to bolster its own research activities and
share in the revenue generated by inventions produced on its own
campus. Faced with inflation, cuts in graduate student aid and
research aid from the federal government, and run-away energy

and other costs, universities understandably see research and development as a means of survival. With the changes in patent law, they will enter into new partnerships with small business in order to financially benefit from discoveries made during federally funded projects. With the new attitudes of the faculty and administration, they will predictably enter into patent and copyright agreements with both big and small business.

With the cutback in federal funding for research, universities will continue to seek out the private research dollar. Also predictable is the continued debate over compromise of academic freedom, conflicts of interest, and possible domination of scientific research by what business defines as important. During this period of confusion and excitement, more refined rules may evolve for guiding the behavior of the university and its faculty.

What States Can Do

While patent policy is set by the federal government, states can do more to stimulate innovation and create new jobs. New York's governor and legislators during the 1981 session agreed to strengthen the New York State Science and Technology Foundation by giving it more of an economic development orientation and appointing two business leaders who have had entrepreneurial experience as officers of small high-tech firms. In addition, the Foundation will operate a revolving loan fund to help meet the borrowing needs of such firms and provide information and referral for those firms needing assistance with management problems.[43]

Minnesota has initiated a state economic development project called "Wellspring." The project uses the university's strengths in biology, agriculture, and engineering to draw corporate support for ongoing and new research and in the process bring new biotechnology industries to Minnesota. The university-related biotechnology center is designed to speed up the movement of technology from the university to industry and be analogous to the agricultural experiment station and the extension service model.[44]

Any state could consider tax incentives or economic development projects designed to encourage partnerships between educational institutions and the private sector. And state scholarships for graduate students in high-demand fields of study would also be valuable. For example, under a plan called MICRO, the state of California will provide $97,500 in fiscal 1982 for one-year graduate fellowships of $12,500 to students studying microelectronics or computer sciences at any of the University of California campuses. The Governor's Office predicts that funding will be increased to $15,000 for the second year.[45]

Similar state efforts may be necessary for New England if the region is to maintain its importance as a sophisticated center of new business start-ups. With intelligent aid from government, New England universities can do even more to strengthen the region's economy.

Taxes and the Donors

While colleges and especially universities benefit from the present federal tax rules governing research contracts and "passive" royalty receipts as well as from the new federal patent law governing university development of a discovery made during federally supported research, campuses will not benefit from the new federal tax rules covering individuals and corporations. President Reagan's Economic Recovery Tax Act of 1981 includes virtual elimination of the estate tax and dramatic reductions in gift, capital gains, and individual and corporation income taxes.[46] Taken as a whole, the bill will provide for tax cuts of almost $750 billion over a six-year period.[47]

Lower Taxes but Fewer Gifts

It is commonly agreed that high-income individuals, who benefit most from these reductions, will choose to pass on a greater share of their wealth to their families. One conservative estimate by the Urban Institute sets the figures at $3.3 billion less in current giving to nonprofit entities for 1982 than if the previous tax rules were in force; $5.5 billion for 1983; $9 billion for 1984; and a total of $17.8 billion overall between 1982 and 1984.[48]

Campuses will experience *most* of this loss because wealthy individuals, typically donors to educational institutions, will face far fewer tax penalties for guarding their wealth. On the other hand, charitable giving to religious institutions will probably increase because lower-income people, typically donors to this group,[49] will be encouraged to give. Those who use standard deductions in computing their federal income tax can nonetheless claim deductions for their charitable gifts. These gifts, on the whole, will go to religious organizations as opposed to cultural and educational organizations.[50]

There is no doubt that the Economic Recovery Act will make charitable giving more "costly" for a person in the higher income brackets. The Act brings a reduction in tax rates on unearned income (from investments, for example) from 70 percent to 50 percent, an across-the-board 25 percent reduction in marginal income tax rates over three years, and a reduction in the capital gains tax rate from 28 percent to 20 percent.[51] What this means is that for a person in the 70 percent tax bracket, the actual out-of-pocket costs of giving a dollar to charity was really 30 cents, because 70 cents would have been captured by federal income taxes and because charitable gifts are deductible in computing one's federal income tax bill. But if the tax rate is pruned to 50 percent from 70 percent, then the price of giving that same dollar rises to 50 cents from 30 cents.[52] Thus giving becomes more "costly."

Likewise, if personal taxes are lower, then there is less need for deductions such as the charitable deduction allowed on appreciation of property given.[53] If estate taxes are substantially lower, then there is also less incentive for the deceased to donate property and thereby enable the executor to deduct 100 percent of the fair market value of the gift from the amount of estate tax due to the federal government.[54]

For corporations, there is also less tax incentive to make charitable gifts. Business income tax has been reduced by allowing accelerated depreciation of equipment and other capital investments.[55] As a slight counterbalance, the Act provides that corporations may claim charitable deductions of up to 10 percent (previously 5 percent) of their taxable income.[56] In short, while the Recovery Act will make more money available for charitable giving, experts predict declines in the actual donations that campuses will receive.[57]

High-Tech and Research Gifts

As mentioned earlier, the Economic Recovery Act provides for a business tax credit of 65 percent of amounts paid to a research university for contract research or 65 percent of corporate grants for basic university research. In addition, a new rule allows a corporation to deduct the cost plus one half of the unrealized appreciation for scientific inventory which is used by higher education institutions for research purposes only.[58]

In order to encourage corporations to donate state-of-the-art high technology equipment, a tax incentive could be established allowing corporations to deduct most or all of the market value of this kind of equipment rather than merely its actual cost. Currently, this equipment is regarded by the deduction rule as business inventory (producing ordinary income) and is not treated as generously as investment property (producing capital gains).[59] Correspondingly, tax incentives could reward corporations for lending out their employees, on a part-time basis, to teach state-of-the-art courses in engineering, mathematics, and other subjects in high schools or colleges. Proponents insist that such an incentive would be a wise public investment because it would quickly address the shortage of teachers in these high-demand fields and enrich the learning and perspectives of students through their contact with actual practitioners. When the shortage was met, the incentive could be revoked.[60]

Tax incentives are an effective, but controversial,[61] way to persuade both corporate and individual donors to contribute to higher education. Because the Economic Recovery Act has pruned away many of those incentives, high-income donors now feel less need to reduce their income and estate taxes through charitable giving. Allowing tax deductions for such contributions means that the government makes a kind of "matching grant" to the campus (in the form of lost taxes) each time that a deduction or credit is taken by a donor. Thus reinstatement of tax incentives or creation of new ones will mean that the federal or state government is also participating in the gift-giving. Needless to say, there are conflicting views on the wisdom of tax incentives for meeting desired goals.

Taxes, Parents, and Students

Students and their parents are granted very few tax breaks now for their payment of the high cost of public college or university education and even higher cost of private education. Students usually are not required to pay income tax on student Social Security benefits, G.I. Bill benefits, and scholarships and fellowships—although the battle continues over whether the higher stipends granted to newly graduated medical students performing hospital residency requirements should be taxed or exempt.[62] Interest payments on loans can of course be used as deductions to reduce a taxpayer's taxable income on federal and most state returns. But because deductions are of more value to taxpayers in higher tax brackets, students and parents of low income do not benefit as much as those with higher income.[63]

In 1954 Congress created the full-time-student dependency exemption which parents may claim if they provide more than half their child's support. Yet the college student can earn more than $750, while usually a dependent cannot. This provision actually allows a double personal exemption: The parent may claim the student as a dependent and in addition the student may claim a personal deduction on his or her return. Repeal of the extra exemption would penalize students who work part-time and during the summer.[64]

As college costs continue to rise, the outcry from middle-income families will predictably intensify. These families cannot qualify for grants and loans designed for low-income students. Yet if these families have more than one child in college, their financial burden can be heavy. Several changes in tax laws may be advisable.

Tax Breaks for Parents

At the state and federal level, arguments are frequently made that parents should be able to enjoy a tax exemption on savings designed for a child's college costs. In New York State parents are now allowed to set aside $750 per year in a special educational savings account in preparation for a child's college costs. If there is more than one child in a family, then each child may be the beneficiary of a separate account.[65] Similarly, proposals are often heard that parents be allowed a tax credit or deduction from gross income for higher education tuition and other costs of their children. A credit is an amount which may be subtracted from the computed tax itself (once net taxable income is determined) whereas a deduction is a subtraction allowed from gross income when the taxpayer is attempting to determine net taxable income.

Opponents of higher education tax credits and deductions from gross income argue that they are both inequitable and inefficient. First, low-income families do not benefit from these because they would be paying little or no income tax. But low-income people who did pay tax would benefit more from a credit. The higher the tax bracket, the more useful is a deduction to be applied to reduce taxable income. Moreover, opponents argue that a state or the federal government could more directly and efficiently provide relief to low- and middle-income families by giving direct grants and loans to the educational institutions themselves so the campuses could hold down tuition costs, and/or by giving more direct grants and loans to the needy students themselves. Direct distribution of money to the institutions or students would be administratively easier than trying to monitor millions of income tax returns. Direct distribution would also preclude the wealthy from benefiting from tax breaks designed for middle- and low-income families. Tax credits and deductions, in short, often grant too much relief to those who do not need help. Instead, governments should block educational deductions and tax loopholes and invest more tax money in student aid programs so that private and public campuses will become more accessible.[66] Nonetheless, it would appear that denying educational tax breaks to those with incomes over $60,000 or setting some comparable ceiling would answer some of these objections.[67]

Amortization of Educational Costs for Students

Some theorists argue that higher education costs should be viewed as a business investment or expense by students rather than, as it is now by state and federal government, as personal consumption. If characterized as a business investment for purposes of creating highly refined skills in order to increase human productivity, then an appropriate response by state and federal tax authorities would be to allow a student to amortize educational costs over his or her expected working life or a set period of that working life. In a similar way, a business allocates and charges to expense the cost of an intangible asset (such as a patent) over its estimated useful life. Thus a student, upon graduation, could each year declare as a business expense one tenth or one twentieth, for instance, of higher education costs accrued. This expense would be subtracted from gross income in order to find the net taxable income.[68] Presumably a student would earn higher income after graduation than before graduation and thus owe higher income taxes.

At the present time IRS allows such a subtraction from gross income for "ordinary and necessary" business expense, but only if the education costs were spent for maintaining and improving skills required by an individual already established in his or her employment, trade, or business or if the employee had to pursue additional education in order to meet the express requirements of the employer or an applicable law or regulation imposed as a condition of employment.[69] In other words, the bias here favors the older worker already established in the work force.

This bias would appear to be unreasonable. Moreover, it seems unreasonable not to allow more liberal deductions as business expense when the advanced, technological market place demands sophisticated skills. Indeed, our complex economy will probably require a worker to upgrade skills several times during a lifetime. Clearly then, these are not educational dollars spent in pursuit of consumption. The more demanding and highly skilled the marketplace, the more necessary, it seems, for state and federal governments to encourage workers to continually invest in acquiring the new skills needed.

An argument against allowing a student to amortize higher education costs is that some element of consumption is involved in a higher education. Because it would be difficult to separate the investment from the consumption, it is wise to leave the Code as it is. After all, students receive the benefit of the educational institution's exemption from property, sales, income, and other taxes. This is a significant public subsidy of higher education across the board. Thus human capital, one expert argues, is already treated as generously as physical capital.[70]

It is probably safe to predict that state as well as federal policymakers will continue to debate this tax break for students. Amortizing a limited amount of higher education costs would seem to be a compromise position. Low- and middle-income parents would benefit from tax-deferred educational savings accounts and tax deductions or credits for higher education costs of their children. But opponents characterize these proposed tax incentives as tax "loopholes" and insist that it is wiser instead to distribute directly more federal financial aid to needy graduate and undergraduate students.

Recommendations

The property tax exemption is a well-deserved benefit for campuses, but states may need to reimburse localities for part of the tax revenues lost. In any case, the public needs to be better informed of how the local community and the state benefit from the presence of campuses.

As a consequence of the new patent law effective July 1, 1981, universities will be able to earn tax-free royalty income from the commercial development of discoveries made by their faculty during federally funded research projects. Realizing the new federal encouragement of innovations and their public use, state policy-makers could move forward to complement the university's new capabilities. This is especially important for New England, whose economy depends on creation of new work through innovation. While it is an exciting time for university research and development, more debate is needed on which models for university involvement are the wisest.

In light of the expected reductions in charitable contributions to campuses brought about by the Economic Recovery Act of 1981, state policy-makers might consider new incentives at the state level for spurring such contributions. Moreover, high technology companies for a limited time at least might be encouraged to aid campuses through donation of equipment and lending of employees to serve as part-time faculty.

Finally, as low- and middle-income parents continue to struggle to meet college costs for their offspring, state and national leaders must give imaginative consideration to their problems. Tax breaks for these parents might be one answer. A more novel approach might be to allow the student, after graduation, to deduct over time a part of his or her educational costs by characterizing them as a necessary business expense. Yet there are those who argue that more federal grants and loans to needy students from middle- and low-income families are preferable to such tax breaks and incentives for either parents or students.

Endnotes

1. John C. Hoy, "An Economic Context for Higher Education," *Business and Academia, Partners in New England's Economic Renewal*, eds. John C. Hoy

and Melvin H. Bernstein (Hanover, N.H.: University Press of New England), pp. 11–12.

2. Robert E. McGarrah, "Expanding Higher Education's Role in New England's Economic Development," *Business and Academia, op. cit.* pp. 124–8.

3. Bruce R. Hopkins, *The Law of Tax-Exempt Organizations* (Washington, D.C.: Lerner Law Book Co., 1977), p. 17. For a discussion of state taxes, exemptions, and revenues raised, see Commerce Clearing House's *State Tax Guide,* Volumes 1 and 2.

4. Section 170 of the *Internal Revenue Code* (St. Paul, Minn.: West Publishing Co., 1981).

5. I.R.C. Section 2055.

6. David G. Brown and Thomas E. Wenzlau, "A View from the Campus," *Public Policy and Higher Education,* eds. David W. Breneman and Chester G. Finn, Jr. (Washington, D.C.: Brookings Institution, 1978), pp. 396–7. Also see *Tax Reform and the Crisis of Financing Higher Education* (Washington, D.C.: Association of American Universities, 1973), pp. 32–36.

7. *Exemption from Taxation in Massachusetts,* printed for the Colleges and Universities of the Commonwealth, Boston, 1910; also see article in October 19, 1939 *Boston Herald* which cites the Cambridge City Council president's complaint that Harvard is "willing to accept everything and give nothing. All the use we are to them is to remove their ashes and garbage and give them police protection on Saturday afternoons at football games." These references appear in Lucy W. Killough, "Exemptions to Educational, Philanthropic and Religious Organizations," *Tax Exemptions* (New York City: Tax Policy League, Inc., 1939), pp. 26–28. Also see complaints from throughout the U.S. which are summarized in William R. Ginsberg, "The Real Property Tax Exemption of Nonprofit Organizations: A Perspective," *Temple Law Quarterly,* Vol. 53, 1980, footnote 5 at p. 293.

8. Proposition 2½ requires a community whose property tax revenues total more than 2½% of the total value of property in the community to reduce taxes by 15% each year until total revenue from property taxes reaches the 2½% level of the total value of property in the locality. For further discussion, see Commerce Clearing House, *State Tax Guide,* Vol. 1, p. 2902 and paragraph 20-519.

9. City of Boston, Office of Fiscal Affairs, "Summary: City of Boston 1981 Fiscal Legislative Submission," January 1, 1981.

10. "White Seeks Fire Service Fee," *Herald American,* December 9, 1981. The legality of such a fee is now being tested in the courts, according to a June 4, 1982 phone conversation with Robert O'Malley, Financial Project Manager, Fiscal Affairs Department of the City of Boston.

11. Ginsberg, *op. cit.,* p. 301.

12. James A. True, unpublished document, Association of Independent Colleges and Universities in Massachusetts, July 1, 1981. According to Ginsberg (*op. cit.,* p. 299), two thirds of the exempt real property in New York State in 1971 belonged to the government, while 80% in New York City was government-owned.

13. Press Release, Massachusetts Taxpayers Foundation, June 10, 1971. The

Foundation's position remains the same, according to a phone conversation with Robert Hughes, Vice President of the Foundation, on June 3, 1982.

14. Killough, *op. cit.*, p. 27; True, *op. cit.*; Ginsberg, *op. cit.*, footnote 33, p. 302.

15. Massachusetts Department of Revenue, valuations as of January 1, 1979. (See Table 7-1).

16. True, *op. cit.* Also see Emil A. Sunley, Jr., "Federal and State Tax Policies," *Public Policy and Private Higher Education*, 1978, p. 397.

17. Ginsberg, *op. cit.*, p. 298; True, *op. cit.*; Henry D. Paley, "Student-Aid Cuts Will Mean Small Savings in U.S. Tax, Big Hikes in State Levies," *The Chronicle of Higher Education*, Vol. 24, No. 6 (April 7, 1982), p. 80.

18. These arguments are presented in "The Universities and the City . . . Facts about Harvard and MIT in Cambridge," a public-relations brochure, 1980; in Killough, *op. cit.*, pp. 28–32; and in True, *op. cit.*

19. "Grants in lieu of taxes on real-property of private colleges and general hospitals," *Connecticut General Statutes Annotated*, Sections 12-20 (a) and (b). Additional explanation provided by Richard Prendergast, Board of Assessment Advisors, Connecticut Department of Revenue Services in phone conversation on April 14, 1982.

20. "Reimbursement for Exemptions," *Maine Revised Statutes Annotated*. Title 36, Section 661. Additional explanation provided in phone conversation on April 14, 1982 with Richard Faucher, Property Tax Division, Maine Department of Revenue.

21. *Massachusetts General Laws Annotated*, Chapter 58, Sections 13-17. Additional explanation provided in phone conversation on April 14, 1982 with Charles Hoen, Bureau of Local Assessments, Massachusetts Department of Revenue.

22. Will Lepkowski, "Research Universities Face New Fiscal Realities," *Chemical and Engineering News*, Vol. 59, No. 47, November 23, 1981, p. 23. "Dupont Gives Harvard Gene Research Grant," *Chemical and Engineering News*, Vol. 59, No. 27 (July 6, 1981), p. 6. Francis X. Campion, "Academe-Industry Linkages of the Biotechnology Revolution: Academe, Industry, and Government Relations," a paper presented at the American Association for the Advancement of Science Convention, Washington, D.C., December 9, 1981.

23. Internal Revenue Code Sections 512(b)(7), (8) and (9).

24. Campion, *op. cit.*, p. 12.

25. Lepkowski, *op. cit.*, p. 24.

26. Campion, *op. cit.*, p. 3.

27. Lepkowski, *op. cit.*, p. 24. Thirty companies each contribute $25,000 annually to robotics research at the University of Rhode Island. See also Lepkowski, "Robotics, A Growing Market that's Getting Crowded," *New England Business*, Vol. 4, No. 9 (May 17, 1982), p. 19.

28. Economic Recovery Tax Act, Section 221. *Explanation of the Economic Recovery Act of 1981* (Chicago: Commerce Clearing House, Aug. 17, 1981), Report No. 11, paragraph 152.

29. Hopkins, *op. cit.*, p. 26.

30. Richard I. Miller, *Legal Aspects of Technology Utilization* (Lexington, Mass.: D.C. Heath Co., 1974), p. 83.
31. Lepkowski, *op. cit.*, p. 23.
32. Lepkowski, *op. cit.*, p. 32.
33. See I.R.C. Sections 512(b)(2) and 511 and 513. Also see discussion by Hopkins, *op. cit.*, pp. 468–9.
34. Arthur A. Smith, "Legislative Developments: Implications of Uniform Patent Legislation to Colleges and Universities," *Journal of College and University Law*, Vol. 8, No. 1, pp. 82–96.
35. Smith, *op. cit.*, p. 92.
36. Campion, *op. cit.*, pp. 10–12.
37. Ann Crittenden, "Universities' Accord Called Research Aid," *New York Times*, September 12, 1981.
38. Jeffrey L. Fox, "Can Academia Adapt to Biotechnology's Lure?" *Chemical and Engineering News*, Vol. 59, No. 41 (October 12, 1981), p.44.
39. Will Lepkowski, "Academic Values Tested by MIT's New Center," *Chemical and Engineering News*, Vol. 60, No. 1 (March 15, 1982), pp. 7–8.
40. Lepkowski, "Academic Values," p. 9.
41. Fox, *op. cit.*, p. 44.
42. Lepkowski, "Research Universities," p. 31.
43. "New York Bills Aim at Stimulating Innovation," *Chemical and Engineering News*, Vol. 59, No. 38 (September 21, 1981), p. 15.
44. Lepkowski, "Research Universities," p. 30.
45. Kim McDonald, "California Pushing Research in Microelectronics," *The Chronicle of Higher Education*, Vol. 24, No. 6 (April 7, 1982), p. 11.
46. Charles T. Clotfelter and Lester M. Salamon, *The Federal Government and the Nonprofit Sector: The Impact of the 1981 Tax Act on Individual Charitable Giving* (Washington, D.C.: The Urban Institute, 1981), p. 3.
47. Explanation of the Economic Recovery Tax Act, *op. cit.*, p. 2.
48. Clotfelter, *op. cit.*, pp. 14–21.
49. *Tax Reform, op. cit.*, pp. 32–36.
50. Clotfelter, *op. cit.*, p. 22.
51. Clotfelter, *op. cit.*, p. 3. Also see *Analysis of the Economic Recovery Act of 1981* (New York: Bender Publishers, 1981).
52. Hopkins, *op. cit.*, p. 26.
53. Hopkins, *op. cit.*, p. 23.
54. Hopkins, *op. cit.*, pp. 22–31.
55. Sections 201, 203, 209 as discussed in *Explanation*, Paragraph 101.
56. Section 263, *Explanation*, Paragraph 334.
57. Clotfelter, *op. cit.*, pp. 14–21; Paley, *op. cit.*, p. 80.
58. Section 222, *Explanation*, Paragraph 156.
59. I.R.C. Section 170 (e).
60. Lynn E. Browne, "Questions and Answers," *New England's Vital Resource: The Labor Force*, eds. John C. Hoy and Melvin H. Bernstein (Washington, D.C.: American Council on Education, 1981), pp. 103–4.
61. Hopkins, *op. cit.*, pp. 23–26; *Tax Reform, op. cit.*, pp. 1–10. Also see Martin Feldstein, "A Contribution to the Theory of Tax Expenditures: The

Case of Charitable Giving," *The Economics of Taxation* (Washington, D.C.: The Brookings Institution, 1980), pp. 99–122.

62. Sunley, *op. cit.*, pp. 281–89.
63. Sunley, *op. cit.*, pp. 311–12; Hopkins, *op. cit.*, p. 26.
64. Sunley, *op. cit.*, p. 288.
65. *McKinney's Consolidated Laws of New York*, Tax Law Section 612 (k).
66. Sunley, *op. cit.*, p. 316.
67. Sunely, *op. cit.*, p. 313.
68. Sunley, *op. cit.*, p. 310. Rhode Island Senator Robert J. McKenna suggested this approach at the Conference on Tax Policy and Higher Education held on January 25, 1982 at the Harvard Club in Boston and sponsored by the New England Board of Higher Education and the Commission on Higher Education and the Economy of New England.
69. I.R.C. Section 662 and Regulation 1.662-5.
70. Sunley, *op. cit.*, p. 311.

APPENDIX:
PATENT RIGHTS IN INVENTIONS MADE
WITH FEDERAL ASSISTANCE

Title 35, Chapter 18, Section 202 (c) (7): of the *U.S. Code:*

In the case of a nonprofit organization, (A) a prohibition upon the assignment of rights to a subject invention in the United States without the approval of the Federal agency, except where such assignment is made to an organization which has as one of its primary functions the management of inventions and which is not, itself, engaged in or does not hold a substantial interest in other organizations engaged in the manufacture or sale of products or the use of processes that might utilize the invention or be in competition with embodiments of the invention (provided that such assignee shall be subject to the same provisions as the contractor); (B) a prohibition against the granting of exclusive licenses under United States Patents or Patent Applications in a subject invention by the contractor to persons other than small business firms for a period in excess of the earlier of five years from the first commercial sale or use of the invention or eight years from the date of the exclusive license excepting that time before regulatory agencies necessary to obtain premarket clearance unless, on a case-by-case basis, the Federal agency approves a longer exclusive license. If exclusive field of use licenses are granted, commercial sale or use in one field of use shall not be deemed commercial sale or use as to other fields of use, and a first commercial sale or use with respect to a product of the invention shall not be deemed to end the exclusive period to different subsequent products covered by the invention; (C) a requirement that the contractor share royalties with the inventor; and (D) a requirement that the balance of any royalties or income earned by the contractor with respect to subject inventions, after payment of expenses (including payments to inventors) incidental to the administration of subject inventions, be utilized for the support of scientific research or education.

Chapter 8

THE ABSENCE OF
NATIONAL POLICY

by John C. Hoy

America no longer dominates the international marketplace in
technological innovation because we have failed to harness the
independent research and training capabilities of higher education
and corporate enterprise. Our national economic policy is uncertain or simplistic; national education policy now floats in the limbo
of lowest priority status. In the face of mounting evidence that
the United States lacks a farsighted national economic development strategy, New England must unite its diverse resources to
forge a commonwealth strategy in support of research and development, education and training as well as regional public service and technology transfer.

John F. Kennedy was the last president who had the vision to
forcefully adopt and implement a national science and technology
policy. Since our massive involvement in the Vietnam War, no
American president has set forth a significant national economic
strategy linking research and development with education and
training. Ronald Reagan's Administration has charted a course and
established priorities that have accentuated and accelerated the
downward trend in national research and development policy; it
seems persistently skeptical that education is deserving of any
status in national policy development, economic or otherwise. The
coming years are likely to mark the trough of this decline. The
reason for anticipating an imminent watershed is the magnitude
of the threat to higher education's stability that we presently face.
The impact of Reagan policies, which only time will fully reveal,

leads to the conclusion that a crisis is near at hand. This crisis will be the product of two decades of inadequate planning.

Record interest rates, record inflation, and record post-war unemployment levels combined with stalemated local, state, and federal expenditures reinforce the conviction that we are confronting a new kind of economic cycle. A profound restructuring of the nation's economic infrastructure is taking place. While American higher education struggles with the impact of all these forces, the backbone of the system has not yet been fully affected. However, an inevitable shake-out will occur in many of our institutions between now and 1990 as the demography of the nation shifts into a period of unprecedented decline in the numbers of young people entering college, and the nation confronts a severe shortage of educated manpower.

The Myopia of Special-Interest Politics

Upon entering the post-industrial era, the U.S. fell victim to an elaborate and confusing legislative process through which government priorities were shaped primarily by highly focused special interest groups. Higher learning increasingly is viewed as just another cause of one of these many single-issue groups. Corporate America is now considered the most effective special interest. Unfortunately, higher education has embraced this cumbersome process along with the narrow vision it implies. This self-imposed myopia has led to intense preoccupation with institutional self-interest and strident defense of the status quo on political issues affecting the academy. The broader public interest too often is forgotten or, at best, endorsed with tired platitudes.

The inherent bias of this method of lawmaking distorts efforts aimed at addressing crucial policy questions by encouraging self-interested debate instead of balanced deliberation. The current battle over federal student financial aid offers an excellent illustration. Legislative leaders who favor federal assistance repeatedly have associated their position with the growing demand for highly educated workers by high technology industry. But they find themselves struggling to recapture the vitality of the arguments presented in the uphill battle waged in the 1960s and 1970s to provide increased access to higher education. Their campus-based allies, as advocates of institutional self-interest, primarily seek to stabilize recent patterns of student market behavior. This process, vigorous as it has become, lacks foresight and neglects the primary element in making its case: the essential requirement that the nation possess a farsighted human capital investment policy.

This impoverishing legislative process cuts many ways. Corporate America's disinclination to lobby effectively in behalf of education and academic research reveals another liability of special interest politics. Corporate America has as much—some might argue more—at stake, for example, in national student financial aid policy than do colleges and universities. But where do corporate leaders stand on this and other issues related to education? Generally behind their well-paid lobbyists, who refuse to acknowledge these broader relationships for fear of blunting an influence honed for narrow corporate issues. And where does academic leadership cast its lot when broad corporate issues of manpower planning and technology development confront the Congress? Other than serving as consultants to congressional committees, academicians engage in such matters from a considerable distance and with increasingly narrow self-interest as the guiding principle in the provision of their counsel.

Fallout from the special interest process rains on collaborative efforts far from Washington, D.C. Manpower planning initiatives remain neglected at the regional level, and communication between higher education and business leaders persists in being inconsistent on issues related to the future supply and demand of educated men and women. The benefit of integrated planning between higher education and growth industries is acknowledged, yet neither sector has been or is currently prepared to risk placing the significant data resources at their command on the negotiating table. While some brokering of manpower training programs has been attempted, and the results are promising, the process has been both tender and tentative, and still must be categorized as experimental. Campus-corporate collaboration frequently is highly touted, but in fact is soft-edged and guarded.

The Potential Legacy of the Reagan Administration

Government by special interest is only one of two major deterrents facing higher education should it seek a new role in economic development planning. The other is fear of massive retrenchment in the federal government's long-term commitment to higher education. This retreat is the single most alarming dimension of Reaganomics. Administration proposals will, if pursued, undercut the best hope for resolution of the nation's most persistent economic problem—inadequate investment in human capital. The Administration's refusal to recognize the significance of the human capital crisis exposes its programs as essentially retrogressive.

As the Reagan Administration struggles with the issues, as it has tenaciously defined them, it is increasingly evident that the single greatest failure of Administration policy rests in an economic development strategy that refuses to acknowledge the technological strength of the American economy. This failure to recognize the role of public investment in human productivity development could be the most damaging legacy of the Reagan years. The Administration has charted a highly ideological economic plan, and it will be unable to shift course even if the powerful arguments taking shape among leaders of our growth industries are successful in forging a new consensus. As any presidential term approaches its midpoint, the possibility of new policy initiatives fades dramatically. In all likelihood the Reagan presidency, rigid as it appears, will be known as one that woefully neglected scientific and technological development at the point when the nation required renewed national investment in education, training, and research.

The United States will have paid an enormous price in the loss of manpower training opportunities if and when the Administration's program demonstrates its effectiveness in controlling inflation. Such control is obviously important, but the cost may be too high. Moreover, the central core of the Reagan program—stimulation of economic growth—remains grievously flawed.

A Regional Policy Imperative

Problems stemming from inadequate federal policies often are compounded by the political judgments of regional leaders. Such is the case with respect to New England higher education, which historically has been the victim of unreasonably frugal public support across the six states. By national comparison, the region has provided cheeseparings and candle ends to its public and private colleges and universities.

The New England attitude probably is due to traditional public policy toward higher education, which has leaned very heavily on the private sector and on initiatives from Washington. The impact of federal spending has ironically been the most significant investment New England has made in human capital policy. New England's long-term reliance upon "capital-intensive labor" allowed the region to reap the benefits of federal programs while not heavily investing resources of its own. Despite the current legacy of this long history of poor public investment in education and research, the complete case for public support has yet to be made in New England, although a new consensus is taking shape. Obstacles remain in many areas. For example, current projections of future training and manpower needs in the region are narrowly based and generally inadequate.

While the region's political leaders have been slow to awaken to this issue, New Englanders understand the nature of the new knowledge-intensive economy which surrounds them. Evidence reveals that the region is leading the nation in the development of the information society and that the young are particularly eager to participate in its development. New England can and should define for itself the meaning of a new federalism aimed at reinforcing the mutual pursuit of economic health in behalf of its people and their institutions. The growth industries, whether sophisticated service corporations or high technology, are interdependent. Information and communications technology by its very nature is not local or parochial. Growth industries are in fact regional, before they are national or global.

New England's New "Information Society"

The information society and the sophisticated service sector it supports are increasingly dependent upon the creation, management, and application of information in such fields as industrial research, health care, finance, insurance, legal services, consulting, and education. The region's manufacturing sector is dependent on the growth of high technology industries, most notably the design and assembly of computers, precision instruments, defense material, and communications equipment that serve as the cornerstone of the information revolution. The minds and skills of people are the region's primary resource in these pursuits.

The most striking aspect of New England's emerging information society is its impact on leadership and decision-making
styles in both the public and private sectors. This is most obvious
in high technology industry, where traditional management methods are giving way to those relying far less on rigid hierarchy and
extreme specialization of individual functions.

Both the leaders and the citizens of the information society are
becoming more versatile—capable of adaptation, critical thinking,
and cooperation with colleagues. Moreover, the leader and the
citizen are more and more often the same; in the information
society, leadership seems to grow both more diffused and more
accessible. This is particularly apparent in New England. As Peter
Drucker pointed out a quarter-century ago, what is really new
in American industry is not the presence of a scattering of "long-
hair" research scientists and engineers, but the emergence of a
workforce in which blue-collar employees are, by historical standards, extraordinarily well educated.

In addition, the New England worker is far more sophisticated
politically than counterparts elsewhere, perhaps because of the
region's town meeting tradition, but certainly because of a higher
level of educational attainment. The mature worker has lived long
enough to know the impact of prolonged industrial decline and
to now sense the economic resurgence the region is undergoing.
The average worker in fact understands the link between business
and education. New England appears to have fully awakened to
the painful realization that its own wealth, political power, and
future prosperity are not based upon natural resources or historic
manufacturing genius. While the region does not fully understand
the complex source of its current vitality and prospects, the case
for a knowledge-intensive future has begun to enter the public
vocabulary, principally through alert interpretation by print and
electronic media.

Constructing a Regional Policy for Education

The rise of the knowledge-intensive economic structure of the
United States may not become the focus of national development
policy for a decade or more. However, in New England the time
is ripe to embrace in a highly public sense the high technology
revolution which has overtaken regional business activity in the

past decade. The change that has occurred in this section of the United States will strongly influence future national economic strategy.

The knowledge-intensive industries of the region carry a significant tax burden and are responsible for whatever health the state treasuries of New England possess. Were it not for the new high technology, New England's economic landscape might resemble Michigan's. Claims upon public policy and policy-makers are being made and will continue to mount in behalf of education and training needs, but these efforts must be better understood in the context of the region's resurgence by citizen and legislator alike.

It is important to note that the new economy still rests on an exceedingly fragile base. New England higher education, from which high technology draws its strength, will face severe problems before the end of the decade. Some of them, such as the anticipated decline in enrollments, will strike New England harder than the nation as a whole. The dilemma demands an imaginative response. A regional redefinition of higher education policy must be forged. Regional, because no single state can effectively meet the wide range of educational, research, and public service needs which will be demanded by a society that has become so economically dependent upon higher education. Regional, because the people of New England are among the most educationally mobile of U.S. population groups and already migrate actively among the six states to pursue their educational and career goals. Regional, because the industries that lead our emerging economy are most often those with a presence throughout the six states. Regional, in that higher education in New England is dependent upon an accreditation network aimed at quality maintenance among the six states.

Public and Private Commitments Required for Educational Excellence

Institutional stability in the 1980s will surely be increased by upholding standards of quality and at the same time exhibiting keener awareness of the manpower needs of the society and its economy. These needs cannot be met, and true quality cannot be preserved, in the face of narrow academic elitism or over-specialized vocationalism. If higher education becomes responsible for building walls between groups of highly specialized experts, or widening the communications gap between the educated and less educated, it will not contribute to greater economic or social productivity. The new information society demands workers trained in a wide variety of complex skills. Because of this broadening of job responsibility, colleges and universities may justifiably exercise caution in giving up general education based on the liberal arts and humanities in favor of an exclusive emphasis on technical training. Leaders in high technology fields increasingly acknowledge the importance of liberal learning as a basis for technology development, most particularly technology transfer.

It has been argued with considerable power in this book that New England's main chance for continued prosperity rests in increased public investment in education and training. The region is at a major crossroads. There is still time to commit ourselves to educational excellence as the backbone of our strategy for economic development. That strategy will require resources the states have not seen fit to allocate historically, but which must be made available now because of the failure of national policy to provide the investment.

Elected leaders have a vital responsibility to fully understand the new link between business and academia, as well as to grasp the importance of the region's educational resources in regional economic terms. The temptation to play out a hand in the political poker games of Boston, Hartford, or Providence statehouse politics as usual may be irresistible. But the risk-taking allure of the New Hampshire lottery, a Vermont turkey shoot, or Maine log-rolling contest will not make New England successful in this complex, comprehensive effort. We are not discussing strategy (pro or con) for a bottle bill or casino gambling. We must address the issue of human capital investment, education, and training and the future of the economy of New England itself—not a piece of the puzzle or a slice of the special-interest pie.

Through a policy of hardfisted investment in human capital development the states may now be prepared to embark upon a new era in support of education and training. In order to maintain New England's preeminence in higher education and high-tech industry, we must now seek to develop the case for active public underwriting, and at the same time bring the resources of the private sector to bear more effectively on a strategy for regional economic development through training programs and academic research. Without additional resources, shared planning, and a commitment from the states to fund new ventures, the region's colleges and universities will remain cautious at best.

Meanwhile, institutions both public and private must continue to meet their broad societal responsibilities. In the present financial crisis, their highest priorities should be the maintenance of quality and the pursuit of excellence in those fields directly and indirectly responsibile for regional economic progress. Policy-makers should aim to fully mobilize and build upon New England's existing educational and research base. Efforts must be made to forge an effective system of higher education, embracing all public and private institutions, ranging from community colleges to research universities. The diversity and autonomy of New England higher education must be respected as a unique national asset. Whether public or private, institutions cannot establish or maintain their identities and fulfill their potential unless they are secure and generally strong. In cases where colleges are lost to enrollment declines or other uncontrollable financial developments, it is imperative that state governing boards be more alert than in the 1970s, possess the expertise to facilitate closure, and protect student and public interests alike. At present, state boards do not possess either sufficient information or adequate powers to serve as more than handwringing witnesses to institutional demise.

Technology Competition: The Political Challenge

On the national level, the country faces a productivity dilemma. The major options for addressing productivity decline focus on technological innovation and the capacity of educated men and women to respond creatively with appropriate concepts, methods, systems, and technology. Keeping federal student aid programs intact, while imperative, is only the first step in meeting these competitive challenges. Next fall's college freshmen will be entering the most productive period of their lives at 35 years of age in the year 2001. Assuring increased, not lessened, educational opportunity for our people is the single most significant national priority for future economic and social health. However, more than this is necessary. The nuts and bolts problems of high technology are as homely in our era as the production of new looms and stitching machines were in the 19th century. The changes modernization has brought about in the organization of work and the value of human labor (however technically challenging this labor has become) require new forms of education and creative analysis by manager and worker alike.

Emulation of Japanese corporate structures is woefully insufficient for Americans and probably doomed to failure here. American requirements call for a deeper and more penetrating response by our best thinkers from many fields, a response built upon American know-how. The challenge requires a national effort reminiscent of the New Deal and the Great Society or the federal response to Sputnik. This effort today will not come from the federal government. The burden rests in the states and regions— with business and industry, higher education, and organized labor. The three groups must gain a mutual perspective to build a coalition in behalf of the region's future. And they must find this common ground rapidly if the public interest is to be served.

Creation of such a coalition need not rely on high-mindedness alone. Evidence of corporate philanthropy in support of higher education, for example, is increasingly recognized as a sign of corporate maturity as well as an expression of calculated self-interest. Labor is increasingly flexible in acknowledging the national economic crisis. The political process will respond to such citizen initiatives. But political leaders themselves will not participate until the necessary concepts, models, and working relationships are in place.

Whatever the final impact of the new federalism turns out to be for New England, new ties among the six states anticipate that this region firmly and rapidly grasp the knowledge-intensive requirements of its own economic future. The major point is clear. Relying on special interest politics-as-usual in the crucial arena of state and regional planning at this time will be inadequate to, if not destructive of, the strategic task before New England.

Three Dimensions of a Human Capital Strategy

In undertaking to strengthen higher education as an asset to New England and making the case for expanded public investment in our colleges and universities, three dimensions are required:

- Making public the hard evidence that academic research and development capability does, in actuality, assure the best prospect for regaining the competitive edge of the regional economy. Specific cases of contributions—large and small—must be documented. Higher education has been all too vague in its presentation of these facts. For a significant minority of citizens, academic research is still distrusted if not feared.
- Increased public awareness that higher education remains New England's "quality" asset, as an "export industry," as a magnet for talented people and for investment, as a responsive system of public and private institutions readily accessible to the region's citizens. Our colleges and universities still project a nineteenth-century image of aloofness and to some a degree of unapproachable arrogance.
- Full acknowledgment that continuing education for New Englanders must attain a level of national and international prominence, in the belief that lifelong creativity and productivity of the region's citizens offers the most promising prospect for continued economic and social development. While increasingly responsive to citizen needs and market demand, higher education in the region has not yet taken a leadership role in elucidating the nature of the regional economy and systematically planning how public and private institutions will efficiently cooperate in addressing future needs.

For New England the pursuit of a human capital investment campaign and its attendant physical capital requirements offers the primary hedge against continued drift in national policy. Furthermore, recent New England economic growth reveals that the case for such expanded investment in knowledge and skills is increasingly compelling to political leaders who are on the receiving end of the new federalism and its proposed trade-offs. Comprehensive solutions to the complex issues facing the nation will be slow to emerge and may blunt the edge of regional priorities. Waiting to serve as handmaiden to the emergence of a delayed national research and development strategy would be foolish in the current political climate, given the specific and urgent developmental needs of New England—needs which will be defined more rapidly here than in the rest of the nation.

Federal Neglect Demands Regional Initiative

While the federal government has faltered to the point of negligence in defining an integral national policy in behalf of scientific research and technological development as well as the related human capital requirements of general education and training, this dilemma does in fact provide considerable latitude to individual states as well as regional coalitions among states to seize the initiative. Whether or not the federal government will be responsive to state-defined economic policies remains untested under the vague terms of the new federalism. However, programs drawn from the experience of specific grassroots models will have a competitive edge in defining and shaping federal priorities when the already overdue debate on science and technology policy begins. Therefore, state and regional policy development takes on an exceptionally significant dimension during this transitional period.

For New England the period is not transitional and the direction to be pursued at this time is obvious. Because a determinedly nonactivist Reagan Administration does not wish to serve as instigator, arbiter, or facilitator of creative models for knowledge-intensive economic development, the responsibility will fall to New England business, higher education, and state government to define the alternatives and implement the plans of action suitable for the region. Since New England is ahead of the rest of the nation in rebuilding its economy through basic and applied research, the region's present position is both perilous and challenging. Passive acceptance of indistinct federal priorities is out of phase with the region's specific opportunity. The peril derives from an historic reluctance on the part of New England institutions to forge the kind of confederation required to supplant, indeed to exceed, federal mandates; a reluctance born out of the post–World War II era of industrial decline and heavy reliance on federal funds and programs.

The challenge confronting New England centers on the independent vision and capacity of state government to collaborate and to plan with business and higher education as full partners. State government in the region must adapt to new modes of active and productive partnerships, and leave its big stick in the closet. To fail to do so will lead to greater intensity of special-interest brawling in the maze of retrogressive policies. If New England applies its available resources creatively, prudently, and cooperatively to the task of economic confederation, we can forge a potent coalition which will powerfully shape the future of national economic policy by example and precedent.

Appendix

A THREAT TO EXCELLENCE
*The Report of the Commission on
Higher Education and the Economy of New England*

Preface

To the New England Board of Higher Education:

In the Spring of 1979 the New England Board of Higher Education (NEBHE) formed a special Commission to explore the relationship between higher education and the economy in the six-state region. The Commission has evolved into a group of 33 prominent citizens representing higher educational institutions, finance, business, organized labor, and government.

Today the Commission is almost three years old. In all of our deliberations we have taken seriously our initial challenge "to raise the consciousness of our leaders and citizenry. . . but also to serve as a kind of watershed that will inform and enrich the activities of the Board."

The accompanying report represents our first effort in attempting to meet this challenge. This report has grown out of over two years of structured review and analysis as well as unstructured and spirited dialogue. Overall, three major seminars have been held and numerous papers commissioned to focus the work of the Commission. Task forces have been created to address the issues of state taxation and its impact on higher education, educational training and industry's occupational demand and the role of higher education in the conduct of state and regional economic policy. The specific results of this ongoing work will be provided to you and the Board in subsequent reports.

However, there is a strongly-held view among Commission members that the time has come to report to the Board on a number of the broader and vital concerns with which New England higher education is now confronted in our region's dynamically changing and growing economy.

A Threat to Excellence has been prepared based on the fundamental belief that New England is the most knowledge-intensive region in the world. Yet, at the same time, Commission members repeatedly have expressed concern about the financial and attitudinal ability of the region's higher education industry to retain this preeminent position in the face of increased competition from other regions. This report elaborates the specific nature of these competitive forces.

All of the Commission members have carefully reviewed the attached report and support its central thrust and specific recommendations. If this report could carry with it a single charge it would simply be that now is the time for New England higher education to focus on the critical relationship between our knowledge-based institutions and the needs of the region's economy.

On behalf of all the Commission members, we submit this report to the Board and our colleagues throughout New England.

James M. Howell
Chairman
Commission on Higher Education
and the Economy of New England

Members of the Commission on Higher Education and the Economy of New England

James M. Howell
Commission Chairman
Senior Vice President
The First National Bank of Boston
Boston, MA

Vernon R. Alden
Chairman of the Massachusetts
 Business Development Council
Boston, MA

Rosalyne S. Bernstein
President
Portland Society of Art
Portland, ME

Roger Bolton
Chairman
Williams College Department of Economics
Williamstown, MA

Russell Brace
President
Diversified Communications, Inc.
Camden, ME

Colin G. Campbell
President
Wesleyan University
Middletown, CT

Laura Clausen
Director of Planning and Resource Development
Commonwealth of Massachusetts
Board of Regents of Higher Education
Boston, MA

Lattie F. Coor
President
University of Vermont
Burlington, VT

Robert W. Eisenmenger
Senior Vice President and Director of Research
Federal Reserve Bank
Boston, MA

Herbert Hollomon
Director
Center for Policy Alternatives
Massachusetts Institute of Technology
Cambridge, MA

John C. Hoy
President
New England Board of Higher Education
Wenham, MA

F. Don James
President
Central Connecticut State College
New Britain, CT

Francis Keppel
Former U.S. Commissioner of Education
Harvard Graduate School of Education
Cambridge, MA

J. Joseph Kruse
Senior Vice President
Textron Inc.
Providence, RI

Sidney P. Marland, Jr.
Former U.S. Commissioner of Education
Hampton, CT

Edward McElroy
President
AFL-CIO Rhode Island
Providence, RI

Donald H. McGannon
Chairman of the Board
Westinghouse Broadcasting Company
New York, NY

Dr. Robert E. Miller
Chairman
New England Board of Higher Education
President
Quinebaug Valley Community College
Danielson, CT

John E. McGrath
President
John J. McGrath & Son
Boston, MA

Robert J. McKenna
State Senator
Newport, RI

John Perry Miller
Institute for Social & Policy Studies
Yale University
New Haven, CT

Frank Newman
President
University of Rhode Island
Kingston, RI

Bruce R. Poulton
Chancellor
University System of New Hampshire
Durham, NH

John C. Revens, Jr.
State Senator
Warwick, RI

Brenda Roberts
Providence, RI

David Starr
Publisher
The Springfield Newspapers
Springfield, MA

Raymond Stata
President
Analog Devices, Inc.
Norwood, MA

William O. Taylor
Publisher & President
The Boston Globe
Boston, MA

Betty Tianti
COPE Director
Connecticut State Labor Council
Hamden, CT

Oliver O. Ward
President
Germanium Power Devices Corp
Andover, MA

Nils Wessel
Immediate Past President
Alfred P. Sloan Foundation
Chebeague Island, ME

Richard West
Dean
Amos Tuck School
Dartmouth College
Hanover, NH

Hilton Wick
President
Chittendon Trust Company
Burlington, VT

I. The Commission's Principal Concern: The Future of Our Region's Higher Education Institutions

The Commission believes that the central task before the New England Board of Higher Education is developing a more complete understanding among all New Englanders of the relationship between the quality of the region's educational system and the performance of the region's economy. Indeed, an underappreciated but important premise of this report is that much of the region's economic success has been due to the incredible diversity, high quality, and broad base of our higher educational institutions.

In many ways, a "critical mass" of institutions of higher learning sets this region apart from others, particularly in terms of its capacity to innovate. Historically, the heterogeneous mix of universities and colleges has enabled the region to adapt to shifting dynamics in the national and even international economy. In recent years, these institutions, collectively, have given the region a competitive edge in technology-based industries, and also have helped to stimulate as well as attract entrepreneurial talent and to encourage new business start-ups.

With 260 colleges and universities, New England is unquestionably the most knowledge-intensive region in the world. The region has 50 percent more institutions of higher education per capita — and nearly twice as many private institutions per capita — than the nation as a whole. Approximately 800,000 students are enrolled in New England colleges and universities. This knowledge-intensity may be a key — if not *the* key — to the future prosperity of New England, for the quality of higher education has far more than a tangential effect on New England's economy.

Institutions of higher education play a strong direct as well as indirect role in the region's economy. With respect to the former, these institutions train people to meet the skilled labor needs of industries within the region for engineers, MBAs, scientists, and other professionals. Furthermore, through their expenditures, educational institutions contribute substantially to the region's economic base and are collectively one of the region's largest employers. New England colleges and universities have direct expenditures of 4.5 billion dollars, generating an estimated 11.25 billion dollars in their overall spending impact on the region's economy. As for their indirect economic impact, common sense suggests — and experience over the years demonstrates — that a good higher educational system attracts people to the region.

During the 80s, both student/graduate preferences and marketplace demands will necessitate institutional adjustments by universities and colleges in response to changing economic requirements. Student/graduate preferences, as measured in a national follow-up study of recent graduates, favor the more career-specific majors — including business, natural sciences, engineering and education. These are viewed as most useful to college graduates.*

With respect to marketplace demands, New England will continue to have a special interest in maintaining a labor force with technology-oriented and sophisticated services skills. Specifically, employment in the high-tech industry accounted for 21 percent of the increase in aggregate New England employment between 1975 and 1980, while job growth in all services (including sophisticated services such as banking, insurance, health, education) amounted to 331,600 new jobs, or roughly 40 percent of the total regional employment increase. Together, the growth in these two sectors alone accounted for two out of three of the region's jobs.

Although the economic impact of professional education has been and will remain particularly important to New England, we cannot overlook the value of traditional liberal arts education to the development and enrichment of the individual and the region. To the extent to which there is a shift in enrollment demand by students for liberal arts degrees in favor of more specific career-oriented professional degrees, as has been the case in recent years, we must find ways to assure a healthy balance of liberal arts programs in professional degree curricula. By the same token we must take steps to include a greater content of technology subjects in traditional liberal arts degrees. As it is, engineers have inadequate cultural literacy and humanists have inadequate technology literacy. Neither situation meets the needs of an increasingly complex society.

As the Commission looks ahead through the 1980's and beyond, the ability of our colleges and universities to remain a positive force in the region's economy through their capacity to educate is no longer assured. At the same time, we are faced with the need to sustain our competitive edge in higher education which has given this region its innovative strength vis-a-vis other regions. Yet, as this report will show, higher education in New England as a basis for regional prosperity is being challenged by higher education in other regions, specifically among the energy-rich Southwest and Western states. This, indeed, is one of the major challenges of the 80's for the region and one which is reflected in the following views expressed by Commission members.

> "Is New England higher education focusing on the critical subjects that are going to shape the future of development? This is the question we ought to be asking ourselves. Are we thinking about and responding to the 'right' areas for education and training?"
>
> "What are the processes by which new thinking gets into the system? Many of our faculty are on the fringes of what were yesterday's scientific advances. How do you take an institution, which through the tenure system gets committed to plumbing, and orient it to tomorrow's engineering?"

---

*Ochsner, N. L., and Solomon, L. C., *College Education and Employment.* Bethlehem, Pennsylvania. The College Placement Council, 1979.

"If officials in higher education attempt to adjust curricula based on an outside view of what we (industry) are doing, their changes are going to be outdated very quickly. Once they catch us in a time frame, we will already be doing something else. We must tell universities and community colleges what our manpower requirements will be."

"As we talk about the need to retrain the increasing proportion of older students in our institutions, we are finding that, in many cases, public policy restricts our ability to address this issue. Many programs which are currently available are almost impossible to use for anyone but traditional full-time undergraduate students. All of our continuing education adult services must, by definition, be 'self supporting,' which places enormous restrictions on the ability of the institutions to address those in more than a haphazard way."

"The varieties of opportunities for training manpower are multitudinous...I am not sure that any one sector (industrial or educational) really knows where all the answers are."

Implicit in all of these comments — and one of the clear areas of Commission consensus — is the need for an ongoing and focused dialogue among business, education, and government to maintain this educational dominance. Public policies, higher education institutional policies, and business policies all have mutually-supportive roles to play in helping colleges and universities respond flexibly to changing industry manpower needs. Moreover, if our competitive educational edge over other regions is no longer assured (or no longer as secure as it has been in the past) — a theme that will be developed in this report — then we will have to move from dialogue among these key participants in the region's economy to collaborative action.

One Commission member urged us to "put out a statement that starts out with the premise that we are a region that lives 'by its wits'." We are, indeed, such a region. Yet a region which has thrived in living "by its wits" must continue to do so, by meeting the challenge of maintaining a flexible, responsive system of higher education. As we look into the decade of the 1980s, this will not be as easy as it has been in the past.

II. The Competitive Strength of Our Knowledge-Intensive Region is Being Gradually Undermined: The Basis for Concern

Over the past two years much of the work of the Commission has been devoted to developing a more complete understanding of the current state of New England's higher education system. As these deliberations evolved, it became increasingly clear that the region's traditionally strong and competitively superior industry — higher education — was facing a number of serious problems. In this section of the report, three of the most significant factors are discussed in detail in order to establish the basis for the Commission's concern.

A Fundamental Weakening of the Public School System

The first factor affecting the competitive strength of the region's higher educational system is a fundamental weakening of the very foundation for higher education — namely, the public school system. Specifically, the public secondary school system has deteriorated measurably over the past decade. Yet, it is virtually impossible to maintain superiority at the college and university level without competent education at the primary and secondary levels. Moreover, students going on to post-secondary vocational education programs must frequently "relearn the basics," diverting resources that could be more productively used for technical training. Finally, for students seeking jobs directly after high school, the public school system must constitute the future backbone of the region's skilled and technical workforce. In all three cases, it is very clear to Commission members that the existing public school system is not fulfilling its goals.

A recent report by the National Assessment of Educational Progress (NAEP), a federally-sponsored project for monitoring the nation's elementary and secondary schools, provides evidence of a sharp decline in reasoning abilities among high school students — and the decline is particularly noticeable in the Northeast. The results of the assessment, which examined and compared reading, science and math achievement for 9-, 13-, and 17-year-olds in 1970-71, 1974-75, and 1979-80 did show that there has been progress in the basic reading skills in the early grades of elementary school. But, the reading, science, and math levels in the high school years — where reasoning and understanding are so important — have declined significantly. The relevant statistical data for in-school 17-year-olds is contained in the table below.*

National Mean Percentages and Changes in Correct
Responses for In-School 17-Year-Olds in Two Reading Assessments

	Years		% Changes
	1971	1980	1971-1980
Total reading exercises	68.9%	68.2%	−0.7%
Literal comprehension	72.2	72.0	−0.2
Inferential comprehension	64.2	62.1	−2.1

While the overall trends in all three categories are a matter of national concern, the most relevant to our discussion here is the deterioration in inferential comprehension. It should also be noted that the rate of decline through

*These and the other data discussed in this section were taken from *Three National Assessments of Reading: Changes in Performance, 1980-81*, National Assessment of Educational Progress, Education Commission of the States, Report NO. 11-R-01, April 1981. Regrettably, the Commission was unable to disaggregate this data by subregions, e.g., for the six New England states. NAEP collects and analyzes the data solely on the basis of the four regions specified above.

the decade actually accelerated. There was a 0.9 percent decline during the first half of the decade, but it accelerated to a 1.2 percent decline in the second half.

The Commission's concerns are also reinforced by the statistical evidence that the most significant deterioration in inferential comprehension has taken place in the Northeast and in the big cities. Note specifically these changes in the data contained in the table below.

Results by Region and Type of Community: Mean Percentages and Changes in Correct Responses for In-School 17-Year-Olds on Inferential Comprehension Exercises In Two Reading Assessments

	Years		% Changes
	1971	1980	1971-1980
Nation	64.2%	62.1%	−2.1%
Region			
Northeast	66.3	62.6	−3.7
Southeast	59.4	59.4	0.0
Central	66.4	63.8	−2.5
West	63.3	62.0	−1.3
Type of Community			
Big Cities	62.5	58.6	−4.0
Fringes around big cities	67.8	65.0	−2.7
Medium cities	64.0	61.7	−2.3
Small cities	63.3	62.2	−1.1

One might not necessarily be alarmed by a national decline of 2.1 percent in inferential comprehension skills over a decade, because there are no guidelines to establish the importance of this decline. However, the differential decline among 17-year-olds in the Northeast vis-a-vis their peers in other parts of the country has disturbing implications for the region.

Finally, some might attribute this differential decline among Northeastern youths to a high percentage of disadvantaged minorities in central city school systems. Yet, this appears not to be the case. Indeed, it is important to note that virtually all of the decline in correct responses in two reading assessments has been among white teenagers. Again, the relevant statistics are shown for in-school 17-year-olds.

Results by Race and Region: Mean Percentages and Changes in Correct Responses for In-School 17-Year-Olds In Two Reading Assessments

	Years		% Changes
Among Whites	1971	1980	1971-1980
Northeast	72.7%	70.8%	−1.9%
Southeast	68.3	70.2	+2.0
Central	72.6	71.6	−1.0
West	69.9	71.6	+1.7
Among Blacks			
Northeast	56.1	56.1	0.0
Southeast	47.7	49.8	+2.1
Central	53.8	54.2	+0.4
West	51.8	50.8	−1.0

The preceding table reveals that in 1971 white teenagers in the Northeast performed better in their reading scores than their counterparts in other regions. By 1980, reading performance among white teenagers in the Northeast had slipped from first to third among the four regions.

Thus, the Commission concludes that there has been a significant decline among the region's high school students in the critical thinking skills that are needed to complete problem-solving tasks in the work place. This decline in critical thinking abilities is especially troublesome as universities and industries seek quality applicants in order to better match industry needs and higher education curricula. If the secondary school systems are not producing as great a body of students who can think critically, then higher educational institutions will be required to use their own increasingly scarce resources to teach skills that should have been acquired in the earlier years. Alternatively, New England's colleges and universities could simply turn away from educating the product of the region. Choosing between such alternatives may well become an unfortunate but necessary reality if our public secondary school system fails to retain its capacity to educate students. As one Commission member pointed out:

> "If New England is going to put its bet on the issue of higher education; that is, its knowledge-intensive base, then it should pay particular attention to the high school situation because it is going to have to build upon it."

A Regional Differential in the Capacity to Finance Higher Education

A second factor affecting the quality of our higher education institutions is a fundamental acceleration in the financial resources available to support and expand academic institutions in the energy-rich states of the Southwest and West, such as California, New Mexico, Oklahoma, Texas, and Louisiana. This development is a direct result of the dramatic rise in world petroleum prices in 1973 and again in 1979. Today, in these energy-rich states, substantially new financial resources have become available directly through the capital appreciation of university-owned, or controlled, oil and gas properties, and indirectly through the recycling of substantial surpluses in the state's severance taxes into publicly-financed higher education.

The swing in this "capacity to finance" higher education in these states is shown in the two region's expenditure rates in the following table. A brief comment about these per capita current funds expenditures is required.* Specifically, the expenditure figures have been adjusted to remove the effects of differential living costs across the states and regions. In this adjustment the U.S. Department of Labor's high family-income budget was utilized.

---

*These data were collected from *Financial Statistics of Institutions of Higher Education,* U.S. Department of Education, National Center for Education Statistics. Capital expenditures are not included in the data.

	U.S.	New England	Oil & Gas States
Real Per Capita Current Funds Expenditures			
By Institutions of Higher Education**			
All Institutions			
1968	$ 83	$108	$ 86
1974	146	160	152
1979	232	243	234
Public			
1968	$ 50	$ 26	$ 62
1974	97	51	115
1979	154	81	177
Private			
1968	$ 32	$ 83	$ 24
1974	49	109	37
1979	78	163	56

A number of interpretative comments may be made to draw out the important conclusions that these data support.

- First, New England remains marginally ahead of the oil and gas states in per capita expenditures for higher education. Nonetheless, there has been a sharp increase in the real current expenditures per capita for both public and private institutions in the oil- and gas-producing states over the period of 1968-1979. This rate of increase, at 172 percent, is nearly 40 percent faster than the increase that took place in New England.

- Second, the differential expenditure rates between the oil- and gas-producing states vis-a-vis New England is due to higher expenditure rates in publicly-supported higher education. Throughout the period of 1968-1979, expenditure rates for publicly-supported institutions in the oil and gas states have been considerably more than two times the expenditure rates in the New England region. Clearly, this is where the competitive commitment and capacity to finance institutions of higher education in the energy-rich states will be most real to New England.

- Third, and as expected, New England expenditures per capita in private higher educational institutions continue to dominate over the country as a whole as well as the oil- and gas-producing states. Unquestionably, this statistical fact underscores the region's preeminent position in private higher education. Spending for private sector colleges and universities in the oil and gas states remains one-third that of their New England counterpart institutions. However, from 1968-1979, expenditures by private higher educational institutions rose 40 percent faster in the Sunbelt than in New England.

**These expenditures are supported by income from *all* sources — public as well as private funds. The analysis of the data on a per capita basis reflects total state population, including the student population.

The relatively high expenditures for publicly-controlled institutions in the Southwest and West is, in itself, a positive development for the nation. What is so disquieting is the potential for stagnation or even deterioration in the financing capacity for publicly-supported institutions of higher education in New England. These institutions will not benefit from the revenue stream of severance taxes that is available to their counterparts in the oil and gas producing states.

Although the preceding table does not provide a breakdown of the expenditure data on the basis of state financial support, a recent study by the National Institute of Education shows the relatively low level of state support for higher education among New England states. For 1980-1981, the national average for state allocation of tax revenue to public higher education was 11.3 percent. The percentage allocation for the six New England states is listed below:

**Allocation of Collected Tax Revenues
to Public Higher Education For Operating Expenses**

	80-81 Percent	Rank Among the 50 States and the District of Columbia
Connecticut	8.4	42
Maine	7.5	45
Massachusetts	4.9	51
New Hampshire	5.6	50
Rhode Island	9.3	39
Vermont	7.5	44
U.S. Average	11.3	

The Commission notes with concern that Massachusetts ranks 51st in state support for public higher education. Indeed, all of the six New England states ranked well below the national average.

Clearly one policy option for increasing the operating expenditures of public colleges and universities in New England is to raise the share of state support. This step can be viewed as a long-term investment, crucial to each state's future economic vitality. However desirable this would be, the tight fiscal position of the New England states may well prevent this from occurring.

The data does not, however, suggest that we need to expand educational capacity in terms of new infrastructure and facilities in publicly-financed institutions. Surplus capacity with respect to physical plant for educational institutions exists throughout New England*. Nonetheless, there is a problem in financing noncapital costs, such as faculty and curricula development in response to changing economic needs in the region.

---

*The major exception is the need for an upgrading and expansion of research and teaching laboratories.

This problem will be exacerbated in the years ahead due to demographic trends; that is, the maturing of the population. The slowing of population growth — especially in older regions like New England — will result in a smaller taxpayer base to support publicly-financed higher education.

Thus, we may conclude at this point by stating that in the decade of the 1970s the oil- and gas-producing states retained a significant lead in spending by publicly-controlled colleges and institutions, while the New England states maintained a dominant position with respect to spending by private higher educational institutions. To be sure, our higher education system as a whole still excels in depth, diversity and excellence, but the gap in spending for all higher education institutions that favored our region in 1968 has almost disappeared.

A Change in the Perception of Economic Opportunity

A third factor that unquestionably impacts on the region's higher educational environment is the perception in this country that New England is no longer the region of greatest opportunity.* The potential consequences of this widely-held view are far-reaching, for once it is believed that a region has lost its economic vitality, it will fail to retain potential leaders, even if it can adequately train them.

In fact, this is proving to be the case for New England, despite the fact that New England is more successful in attracting new college students than any other region in the country. Indeed, New England's in-migrating students comprise 24.6 percent of new enrollments; Vermont, New Hampshire and Rhode Island rank third, fourth, and fifth respectively in the country in net in-migration at post-secondary institutions.

Moreover, in the decade of the 1970s, New England institutions of higher education have performed in a generally positive and responsive manner in providing training for those skills in greatest demand by the technology-based growth industries in New England. The New England performance is especially noteworthy in the area of engineering students. The region substantially outperformed both the nation as a whole and the oil- and gas-producing states in the generation of engineering and business degrees. The relevant data are shown in the following table.**

Earned Bachelor Degrees by Region Per 10,000 Persons
Area of Academic Specialization

	Business & Management			Engineering		
	1971-72	1976-77	1979-80	1971-72	1976-77	1979-80
New England	6.26	8.31	10.50	3.27	3.30	4.08
Oil- and Gas-Producing States	5.55	6.59	7.39	2.24	1.86	2.82
U.S. Total	5.92	7.01	8.24	2.47	2.24	3.04

*For documentation of the broad support for the view that Southern states provide a more positive climate for investment and employment, see the detailed survey results in *The Dynamics of Interaction Between Government, Business and Labor in the Northeastern United States*; Yankelovich, Skelly and White Inc., June 1981. Respondents in the Southern states provided a control group for this assessment of regional perceptions of opportunities.

**The source of these data is "Earned Bachelor Degrees Conferred by Institutions of Higher Education", U.S. Department of Education, National Center for Education Statistics.

Equally encouraging findings are contained in the forthcoming book, *New England's Vital Resource: The Labor Force.** For example, although New England educates 6 percent of the nation's students, the region trains approximately 8 percent of the country's undergraduate engineers. Moreover, in 1979 and 1980 the number of women earning A.B. degrees in engineering in New England has grown by a third. During these years, the increase was one-fifth nationally, so the region outpaced the U.S. in growth.

Notwithstanding these favorable statistics, the region's higher education institutions still are not keeping pace with the demand for technical professionals in the region. High-technology firms in New England as well as throughout the country are reporting shortages of engineers, computer scientists and managers with technical backgrounds, and it is argued that these shortages will persist for the foreseeable future.** The problem is caused largely by an inadequate educational capacity in these areas. For example, the "capacity crunch" that exists in engineering is due to an unprecedented gap in salaries for engineering faculty in comparison to industry positions. Unless greater financial resources are forthcoming to close the salary gap and to fund badly-needed equipment for research and teaching labs, the shortage of technical manpower will "squeeze down" the growth of the high technology industry which is so vital to the New England economy. Indeed, the implication for the region's economy is significant, inasmuch as companies tend to locate and expand where technological resources — skilled labor in particular — can be found.

Why should this be a concern to the region's educators? Just as the output of educated individuals affects a region's prosperity, so the prosperity of a region ultimately will affect the ability of these institutions to produce educated individuals. Furthermore, a region that loses ground economically is less likely to provide the resources to maintain its cultural amenities — often a critical factor in attracting students from outside the region. It is this mutually-supportive relationship between higher education and the region's economy that makes the loss of leadership a concern to those who are seeking to maintain the quality of New England's colleges and universities.

Contrast today's situation with that of two to three decades ago, when the Eastern Seaboard was viewed as *the* area of real opportunity. While the region has made an almost unparalleled recovery through high-technology growth and old mill-town revitalization, this region simply does not draw young trained people from other regions seeking advancement as it once did and is not "holding onto its own."

That New England has historically excelled in higher education has meant that educational attainment and economic opportunity co-existed in the region.

---

*To be published by The American Council on Education and the New England Board of Higher Education in March, 1982.

**Yet, in a recent NEBHE survey of 400 New Englanders who are leaders in government, higher education, business, and labor 67 percent of the respondents considered high technology to present "the greatest opportunities for economic growth and stability in New England in the 1980's."

Now this is beginning to change, and a recent study on place of birth and place of business success provides some dramatic insight into this issue.

Specifically, the study shows that in 1951 approximately 44 percent of all Southern-born business leaders pursued their careers in the North, whereas in 1977 only 20 percent did so.* The study also revealed that in 1951 about 21 percent of the business leaders who pursued their careers in the South were born in the North. Today this has increased to 25 percent. Thus, the North is "losing the battle for business leadership," with a considerable percentage of Northern-born leaders migrating to the South and, at the same time, the Southern-born business leadership showing a dramatic geographical career preference for the South. The relevant statistical comparisons are shown in the following table.

Region of Birth and Region of Career

	1951 Study	1977 Study
Birth in South, Career in South	55.9%	79.4%
Birth in South, Career in North	44.1	20.6
Birth in North, Career in South	19.8	23.6

There are many complex factors that may account for these regional shifts in the perception of economic opportunity, but a factor that must be recognized as significant is the disparity in living costs in the North and South. A recent study carried out by The First National Bank of Chicago** reveals clearly that regional differences in living costs and taxes can and do dramatically influence the real disposable income situation of individuals.

Shown in the table below are the average differential (the U.S. average is the norm) regional living costs, state and local tax burdens per capita, and median family income for the six New England states and thirteen Sunbelt states. (The basic data input is disposable per capita income by state for 1975.)

Living, Tax, and Income Differentials
In New England Relative to the Sunbelt

	New England Differential
Average differential living costs per capita	+ 117.5%
Average state and local taxes per capita***	+ 33.6%
Median family income	+ 13.4%

---

* James M. Howell, "Shifting Patterns in Southern Business Leadership" *Review of Regional Economics and Business,* October, 1979, pp. 3-9. These statistics represent a significant percentage of regional business leadership — those whose names appeared in the *Who's Who in Commerce and Industry,* a standard biographical reference work that includes roughly 18,000 names nationally.

** "Is Alabama Richer Than New York?" *First Chicago World Report,* The First National Bank of Chicago, May, 1977.

*** Services that traditionally have been financed by state and local taxes in New England are more likely to be financed privately in the Sunbelt, thus accounting for part of the cost of living differential. Moreover, qualitative variations in service that cannot be quantified are not reflected in these cost of living figures.

Unquestionably, disparities of this magnitude will not go unnoticed as individuals plan their careers.

While the cost of living disparity contributes to an out-migration of professionals from the region, demographic trends alone within the region foretell the likelihood of potential labor shortages.

- The region's share of the 15-24 year age group is declining slightly more than that of the nation as a whole, but much more rapidly than the Sunbelt states. Consequently, New England will have a smaller proportion of youngsters graduating from its school systems — and entering the labor force — than the Sunbelt states.

- The average age of industrial workers in the region's manufacturing sector is in excess of 55 years. This important regional labor source will be joining the ranks of the retired during the decade of the eighties. Thus, labor shortages at the technical and skilled levels will become even more commonplace.

One has to acknowledge, however, that there is a positive side to the perception of the region's economy. A major regional strength can be found in the presence of R&D talent and facilities — particularly within the Greater Boston area — and the area's attractiveness to technology-based firms, potential entrepreneurs and those seeking a research-oriented career. New England's strong R&D base is not a new or recent phenomenon:

> Industrial research in machinery and instruments has been conducted in this region since the middle of the nineteenth century, and many of today's research-based firms owe much of their advantage to the accumulated firms which came before them. The robotics industry, for example, came out of a long line of New England machine tool development. In recent years robotics has been advanced by input from computer research, in particular from computer-aided manufacturing (CAM) developments which were themselves designed as an input for manufacturing firms. It is this total environment of industries and universities together making new products and processes in fields of common interest which provides a basis for high technology development.*

Continued growth in R&D spending may well be one of the more hopeful signs for the future economic vitality of the region.

Another potential, but generally unexploited strength, may be found in the expanding opportunities for employees to pursue advanced degrees while remaining on-the-job. Such opportunities not only help provide a more productive regional economy by keeping professional workers and management up-to-date on technological advances, but also can serve as a major industry recruitment tool for attracting skilled and semi-skilled workers. Higher educational institutions can respond to these opportunities by providing flexible programs to upgrade their labor force skills.

We may summarize by stating that these three pressure points will weigh heavily on the competitive educational edge our region has vis-a-vis other

---

*John S. Hekman and John S. Strong, "The Evolution of New England Industry," *New England Economic Review*, Federal Reserve Bank of Boston, March/April 1981.

parts of the country: (1) the decline in our public secondary school system; (2) the increased capacity to finance higher education in the energy-producing sates; and (3) a changing perception that the North is no longer the region of opportunity. Collectively, these factors add up to a negative trend in the region's "capacity to educate." Moreover, even if the magnitude of this trend does not appear to be significant, the direction does not augur well for the region's economy.

Reversing this trend constitutes a clear and direct challenge for educational, business and government leaders if we are to maintain a positive relationship between the region's institutions of higher learning and the needs of the New England economy. Our region can — and must — meet this challenge head on.

Recommendations: Regaining the Competitive Strength of Our Knowledge-Intensive Region

1: Recommendations to Overcome the Perceived Weakening in the Public Secondary Schools

The foregoing analysis of New England's competitive economic condition provides strong evidence that the young people in our high schools are not learning as they should, either in absolute or comparative terms. Without attempting to place the blame for this condition (educators, family, social environment, changing values, etc.) we see the secondary schools as critically essential to the strategies of insuring a favorable economic future for the New England states. While much of this analysis and the corresponding recommendations apply, appropriately, to our colleges and universities higher education relies primarily upon the flow of able young people from the secondary schools.

Of equal importance to our future New England economy (though only tangentially treated in this document) is the flow of able and employable young people, not college bound, into the work places. It should be noted that, in general, one-half of our high school graduates will pursue college, the other half will move immediately to work.

High school educators, including administrators and teachers, are urged to look upon the recommendations that follow, not as "another attack," but rather as a collegial expression of shared concern and long overdue readiness to help. Given the long view, the high schools and their communities are at least as dependent upon a viable economic future in the region as are the colleges — if not more so. And, their contributions to that future are crucial.

- **Expanded outreach to secondary schools in New England's urban centers should be undertaken by individual universities and colleges.**

Higher education has neglected its significant responsibilities for the quality of secondary education within the region, especially in the older cities. Coordinated, long-term effort is now required to redress the deterioration of achievement and standards, such effort to be mutually conceived and carried out by high school and higher education officials.

- **An assessment of teacher certification procedures should be carried out in each of the six states, including a review of legislative constraints.**

Certification standards for teachers in secondary schools should be reviewed on a regular basis. Flexible standards should be permitted in cases where individuals have demonstrated their proficiency apart from the formal classroom. This condition has particular relevance to the fields of mathematics and technology, where grave shortages of qualified teachers are an increasing problem.

- **Senior personnel officers of major New England corporations should assist high school staffs in a periodic review of high school curricula, notably in fields relating to business and industry.**

The purpose of this review would be to maintain a level of technical information/training in high school classes compatible with the evolving realities of the workplace. This review would be undertaken as part of the normal curricula reforms carried out by state or local education agencies.

- **Follow-up evaluation and assessment procedures for teachers should be developed and implemented on a state-by-state basis.**

While the Commission acknowledges the difficulties inherent in the competency testing of teachers, performance evaluation in some form should be provided on a systematic and continuing basis. State commissioners of education should develop teacher evaluation and assessment techniques. Where weaknesses are identified, constructive assistance should be afforded, through the willing engagement of business and higher education resources.

- **The secondary schools should appeal to business and industry for key personnel to augment the teaching of mathematics and science. Industry should promptly respond.**

The National Assessment of Educational Progress (NAEP) findings cited in our report clearly show a decline in reasoning skills among high school students, especially in the areas of mathematics and science. To help overcome this shortage, business should find non-traditional ways of involving itself in the educational process, for example, loaning technical experts to reinforce the teaching of high school computer courses. The disparity between the salaries of teachers of science and mathematics and individuals with corresponding skills in business and industry could also be ameliorated through this process. Part-time positions for such teachers in industry should be considered, affording them improved income, without requiring them to permanently leave the classroom.

- **Vocational education should be strengthened through the development of model programs involving "hands on" experience in actual work settings.**

These programs should be based on an assessment of occupational skills in demand after a review of Divisions of Employment (DES) Security and other relevant labor data by a task force of school officials, representatives of vocational education, business representatives, labor market specialists and college faculties.

- **Partnerships between individual high schools and individual corporations should be systematically established in all states.**

These partnerships should build upon the successful models, now in place around the country. Examples may be found in programs launched by Security Pacific Bank in California; General Electric in New York City; The Trilateral Partnership in Boston; and, the Bell System in Bridgeport and New Haven, Connecticut. What these programs have in common is loaning company professionals to teach or work with students in secondary public schools. A key element of such programs is the "model" building that occurs, especially for disadvantaged students.

2: Recommendations to Overcome A Regional Differential In the Capacity to Finance Higher Education

One of the most significant findings that emerged from the Commission's research and deliberations is the extent to which higher education is a growth industry. Indeed, New England's recent economic advances have been built largely around high technology, in which the region's colleges and universities have played a vital role.

If higher education is a regional growth industry, it ought to be treated as such. State tax policies should encourage private sector contributions to higher educational institutions. State policies also should promote flexibility in curricula and staffing that is responsive to business needs. Moreover, financial support for higher education among the six New England states should be increased. As a member of the Commission pointed out: "If we are going to do anything about our competitive situation we need to get a more enlightened perspective on the value of our public investment in education."

An important forum for assuring "the value of our public investment in education" is the state legislature. Yet, there are other important avenues by which public as well as private resources can be used more effectively to enhance the future of higher education as a public investment and as a growth industry: collaborative planning among key participants in the university and college systems within and among the New England states; and cooperative arrangements between educational institutions and industry through which firms would loan equipment and personnel and provide work scholarships to students.

A common theme in the recommendations that follow is that cooperative planning and new collaborative arrangements among educators, government officials and business leaders can help "stretch" our limited educational resources much further. Another major theme is the need to improve the capacity of colleges and universities to provide technology-oriented skill development. However, many Commission members emphasize that skill development does not imply exclusively vocational skills, but also "the capacity to be well-developed people capable of having independent thought."

- **Industries in the region, especially in the high-tech field, should join together to finance "work scholarship" contracts at the college and university levels.**

  Under such a program, a consortium of industrial firms would guarantee a certain number of loans to support young people whom they wish to employ following the completion of their courses. Upon graduation, if a student works for a specified period for a company in the consortium, the loan would be regarded as a work scholarship and forgiven. Should a student decide to work elsewhere, his/her loan would have to be repaid to the consortium of companies participating in the program.

  The advantage of this approach is that it requires industry to pay for expanded university training services to meet the needs of companies in the region while, at the same time, requiring institutions of higher education to provide the necessary technical curricula.

- **Cooperative arrangements should be initiated through which colleges and universities can use state-of-the-art industry equipment on "off-hours."**

  These kinds of arrangements would offer short-term, temporary expedients for the problem of equipment and faculty shortages. Over the long run, however, colleges and university officials should work with business and government officials on plans to update the educational infrastructure (laboratories and state of the art equipment) for engineering and computer science fields.

- **Five-year state plans for higher education should be undertaken in each of the New England states. Massachusetts should build on the five-year planning process of the state Board of Regents.**

  Business, labor and higher education leaders — representing diverse labor market areas — should serve on working groups which formulate and supervise the implementation of these plans. These working groups should discuss specific manpower data, emerging manpower needs, and new mechanisms for financial support. Once formulated, the plans prepared by these working groups should be reviewed annually to take into account changing industry needs.

- **Colleges and universities should initiate "quality" reviews of their programs.**

  If higher education is to be treated differently in state tax structures, educators must acknowledge that it is essential to measure the quality of degree programs in their institutions. Toward this end, these institutions ought to examine the New York State process whereby a council consisting of educators, both out of state and in-state, assesses the quality of Ph.D. level programs in public and private universities.* The New York State effort has resulted in a university self-examination process leading to a reduction in the number of weak programs and more resources for other program areas.

- **Public and private colleges ought to pool common resources and eliminate curricula redundancies, as well as provide new curricula and flexible staffing patterns in response to industry needs.**

Just as the five-year planning process would provide incentives for intrastate cooperative planning, new incentives are needed for interstate planning among educational institutions. While acknowledging that universities and colleges must — and will continue to — compete for students and faculty, it is important, nonetheless, that in a period of scarce resources, these institutions collaborate on long-range planning.

The region should expand and build upon some of the efforts in cooperative planning that are already underway. A notable example is the five college consortium of Amherst, Smith, Mount Holyoke, Hampshire, and the University of Massachusetts. This experiment could be adapted by public and private institutions throughout New England.

- **The community college system ought to concentrate on providing skill development for technical careers while still attempting to meet students broader educational needs.**

The Commission fully recognizes the special role of community colleges in expanding opportunities for a broad segment of the population. Yet, community college programs should be adjusted to simultaneously meet the skilled employee requirements of high-tech firms and companies in the sophisticated service sector as well as the educational needs of this segment of the population. Curricula emphasis should be more vocationally-oriented, focusing on industrial training (e.g., machine operators) and office services (e.g., accounting, data processing) at the skilled and semi-skilled worker level. The "track record" of the vocational/technical system in New Hampshire demonstrates that such programs can operate successfully.

- **Universities and colleges should cooperatively develop the regional case for support from the private sector, including foundations and corporations.**

Corporations, because of the benefits they receive, directly and indirectly, from colleges and universities in the region — such as employing their graduates — have a responsibility to understand the needs of institutions of higher learning for financial support. Specifically, higher education institutions should seek challenge grants from foundations which can be matched by corporations. Such initiatives should be taken cooperatively as well as individually by colleges and universities.

---

*New York State Board of Regents, Doctoral Evaluation Project, University of the State of New York.

- One-on-one relationships should be established between individual companies and individual educational institutions enabling professionals to serve as part-term faculty at local colleges.

    The purpose of this recommendation is to help overcome the difficulty experienced by colleges in attempting to hire quality teaching staffs in technology-oriented subjects and sophisticated services as enrollments in these fields increase. As an outcome of college/company discussions, a firm could make available skilled individuals who would be paid to provide part-time instruction in subject areas mutually determined by industry and the college.

- Colleges and universities should increase their sponsorship of contracted training and education programs for business and industry.

    A recent market study undertaken by the University of Massachusetts reveals that employers need and want contracted in-plant education and training programs in far greater numbers than local colleges and universities are providing them. Yet, structural and administrative difficulties complicate the current situation. One possibility for overcoming these problems is the creation of — or designation of — a group that could identify course needs of employers, potential instructors within local corporations, and colleges prepared to sponsor and certify courses. Such a group could then help match business and industry labor training needs with college and university training capacity.

3: Recommendations to Improve the Perception of New England as a Region of Opportunity

As the Commission's report indicates, New England continues to be more successful in attracting new college students than any other region in the country. However, living costs that are out of line with the national average and the perception of greater opportunities elsewhere are discouraging students from remaining in the region after graduation.

Yet, the performance of the New England economy — particularly in the areas of high technology and sophisticated services — has been most impressive. Indeed, the central focus of the following recommendations is for the region to "accentuate the positive," to tell its story to a broader audience, and to encourage a new way of thinking about New England, within as well as outside the region.

The communications campaign envisioned in the recommendations that follow is one in which key participants in the region's economy — including academic institutions, business firms, and state governments — have a major stake. Accordingly, a commitment to play a role in improving the region's image is required on the part of each of these participants.

- The New England Board of Higher Education, in conjunction with the six state governors, should launch a joint effort to publicize the attractiveness of the region as a place to study, work and live.

Given the highly favorable economic forecast for New England in the 1980s - as documented, for example, in a recent report by the Joint Center for Urban Studies of MIT and Harvard University entitled "Regional Diversity" — we can justifiably laud the virtues of the region. The economic and cultural vitality and knowledge-intensive structure of New England society should be presented vividly and cooperatively by the New England Board of Higher Education and the governors as a priority initiative on behalf of continued regional development.

A strong region-wide commitment directed toward attracting and keeping students, skilled workers, and talented graduates in New England should be the focus of this effort. A communications campaign along these lines would help to build an appreciation of our strengths within as well as outside the region.

To this end, the Commission recommends that funds be raised to establish an ongoing communications campaign and support services. One possibility is that the New England Board of Higher Education, working with the governors, request that business firms, state governments, and universities donate one-half of one percent of their public information budgets which can be pooled to support regional promotional programs.

The Commission notes that all universities and colleges in Rhode Island have jointly funded, designed and published recruiting material for the state. This kind of effort — on a broader regional basis — is envisioned in this recommendation.

- **The interdependent relationship between the region's educational capacity and the success of business firms located here should be documented as a major component in the publicity campaign recommended above.**

Specifically in the area of research and development activity, New England has a concentration of colleges and universities unequalled in other regions and, in the words of one Commission member, "Ph.D = R & D". The linkages between this academic R & D activity, corporate R & D activity, and the international preeminence of many regional business firms has not been — but ought to be — clearly established. The Commission calls upon the Massachusetts High Technology Council (MHTC) to document this relationship based on the experience of MHTC firms.

- **Institutions of higher education in the region should demonstrate innovative techniques which could be used especially to retrain established mid-career workers for occupational skills that are in demand by industry.**

Retraining is needed for workers whose jobs have become obsolete, and would be particularly valuable in assisting government workers who have lost their jobs as a result of cutbacks in federal, state, and local budgets. Upgrading is equally important, enabling workers to improve their vocational skills and enhance their earnings capacity. The availability of both effective retraining and upgrading programs would help to confirm the view that the region is an area of economic opportunity.

Finally, the presence of an older work force — cited in this report — need not be viewed as a regional economic disadvantage. Indeed, as one Commission member — representing a high tech-firm — pointed out, "Having an aging population is viewed by my company as a regional advantage because of the stable skill level of the work force. We are concerned about not having enough young people, but the maturity of the work force need not be strictly a negative."

A Call to Action: The Next Step

The Commission stands ready to work with leaders from state government, education, and industry who will be called upon to implement the new policies and programs contained in the preceding recommendations. Toward this end, we believe that an ad hoc committee should be created, composed of members from each of the six state legislatures, including members of the finance, education, and appropriations committees. As a first step, this committee should hold public hearings in every state in the region on the issues raised in this report. Business and industry leaders should participate in the hearings to demonstrate the important role of higher education in the region's economic growth.

A central goal of the hearings should be identifying ways in which the public and business sectors can facilitate the contributions of higher educational institutions to economic development in the region. One agenda item would be financing the costs of higher education — faculty and curriculum development in particular — in response to changing economic needs. Specifically, state tax systems can be used more creatively to strengthen the higher educational system. Among the options that might be considered are earmarking a portion of the business profits tax for expanding the engineering capacity of New England colleges and universities, both public and private; and special tax treatment — or preferably matching grants — for corporations that make contributions to educational institutions in terms of staff, facilities, and equipment.

The hearings should also identify "planning disincentives" that affect publicly-controlled higher education, and which ought to be removed. A disincentive cited by college and university officials is that savings in one part of a public college/university system cannot be reallocated to other areas. Instead, those savings must be returned to the state. This situation prevents publicly-controlled universities and colleges from applying savings to upgrade staffing, facilities, and equipment in newly-emerging technical fields.

The Commission fully expects that these hearings will also deal with a situation that one Commission member termed "a state of emergency": alleviating the shortage of high school mathematics and science teachers through modified certification standards and differential salaries.

An important outcome of the hearings would be a broad base of support for new policies and actions that are regarded as priority concerns. Equally important is a mutual understanding of how leaders from education, industry, and state government can participate in this process, collaboratively working to strengthen the relationship between New England's higher educational institutions and the region's economy.

INDEX